ALCTS Papers on Library Technical Services and Collections, no. 7

Bibliographic Control of Conference Proceedings, Papers, and Conference Materials

from the
Preconference on the Bibliographic Control of Conference Proceedings

at the
Annual Conference of the American Library Association
June 24, 1994, Miami, Florida

sponsored by

Association for Library Collections & Technical Services
Cataloging and Classification Section
Committee on Cataloging: Description and Access

and

Association of College and Research Libraries
Science and Technology Section

edited by
Olivia M. A. Madison
and
Sara Shatford Layne

series editor
Edward Swanson

Association of College and Research Libraries
A Division of the American Library Association
Chicago 1996

The paper used in this publication meets the minimum requirements of American National Standard for Information Sciences–Permanence of Paper for Printed Library Materials, ANSI Z39.48-1992. ∞

Library of Congress Cataloging-in-Publication Data

Preconference on Bibliographic Control of Conference Proceedings,
(1994: Miami, Fla.)
Bibliographic controlof conference proceedings, papers, and
conference materials from the Preconference on the Bibliographic
Control of Conference Proceedings at the annual conference of the
American Library Association June 24, 1994, Miami, Florida / edited
by Olivia M.A. Madison and Sara Shatford Layne.
p. cm. -- (ALCTS papers on library technical services and
collections ; no. 7)
Includes bibliographical references and index.
ISBN 0-8389-7860-6
1. Cataloging of conference proceedings--United States-
-Congresses. I. Madison, Olivia M. A. II. Layne, Sara Shatford.
III. American Library Association. IV. Title. V. Series.
Z695.25.P74 1994
025.3'4--dc20   96-30103

Printed in the United States of America.

00 99 98 97 96   5 4 3 2 1

Contents

Contributors to this Volume

Karen Baschkin, Vice President and Manager of Acquisitions Department, InterDok Corporation (Harrison, New York).

Daniel W. Kinney, Assistant Head, Cataloging Department, Main Library, SUNY at Stony Brook (Stony Brook, New York).

Olivia M. A. Madison, Assistant Director for Public Services, ISU Library, Iowa State University (Ames, Iowa).

H. Robert Malinowsky, Head, Collection Development, Main Library, University of Illinois at Chicago (Chicago, Illinois).

Loren D. Mendelsohn, Chief of Public Services, the Library, City College of New York (New York, New York).

Mary Page, Head of Technical and Automated Services Department, Library of Science and Medicine, the State University of New Jersey, Rutgers (Rutgers, New Jersey).

James A. Ruffner, Collection Development Officer, Science and Engineering Library, Wayne State University (Detroit, Michigan).

Sara Shatford Layne, Head of Cataloging, Science & Engineering Library, UCLA (Los Angeles, California).

Beacher Wiggins, Chief, Arts and Sciences Cataloging Division, Library of Congress (Washington, D.C.).

Introduction

Olivia M.A. Madison and Sara Shatford Layne

Background

Conference proceedings are universally acknowledged as troublesome publications, but at the same time, they are regarded as particularly important publications in the sciences. Because of their valuable but problematic qualities, in 1984 the Science and Technology Section of the Association for College and Research Libraries appointed several groups to address different aspects of conference proceedings, including their bibliographic control. One of these groups, the ad hoc Committee on Designing a Conference Proceedings Style Sheet, addressed bibliographic control problems at their source by preparing "Recommendations for Publishers of Conference Proceedings", which appear as Appendix B of these proceedings.

In 1987, as a result of a recommendation from the Task Force on Subject Access to Science Materials, the Science and Technology Section established the Committee on Subject and Bibliographic Access to Science Materials. To this committee devolved the responsibility for STS concerns relating to the bibliographic control of conference proceedings. Generally these concerns fall into three categories:

    1) concern for the producers of the proceedings;
    2) concern for the utilizers of the proceedings; and,
    3) concern for the catalogers of the proceedings.

The first concern has already been addressed by the "Recommendations" referred to above, but in addition, the committee currently is exploring the possibility of turning the Recommendations into a formal standard, perhaps even an international standard. The second concern, for those who utilize the proceedings, was addressed by writing the "Guide to Searching the Bibliographic Utilities for Conference Proceedings," which was published in 1994 by ACRL. Joan Lussky, a member of the committee, suggested that the best way to address the third concern, the concern for the catalogers, would be to hold a preconference on conference proceedings that would include practical as well as theoretical components. With this suggestion, made some four years ago, the Preconference on the Bibliographic Control of Conference Proceedings was conceived. In 1990, the STS Council approved the idea of such a preconference in principle and agreed that it should, ideally, be sponsored both by STS and by the Cataloging and Classification Section of the Association for Library Collections & Technical Services. ALCTS CCS was approached late in 1990, and Marilyn McClaskey, the chair at that time, was enthusiastic about the idea and delegated it to the Committee on Cataloging: Description and Access within ALCTS CCS. Because preconferences for 1993 were already in the planning stages, the Preconference on the Bibliographic Control of Conference proceedings was scheduled for 1994, and in the spring of 1992 the planning committee for the preconference was formed, with four members from STS and four from CC:DA, including a co-chair from each section. The final committee membership consisted of the following individuals:

> Olivia M.A. Madison, Co-Chair (CC:DA)
> Sara Shatford Layne, Co-Chair (STS)
> Daniel W. Kinney (CC:DA)
> David Mill (CC:DA)
> Colby Mariva Riggs (CC:DA)
> Nirmala Bangalore (STS)
> Joan Lussky (STS)
> Rebecca Uhl (STS)
> Sarah Mitchell (volunteer consultant)

Preconference Planning Committee's activities

The first set of decisions that needed to be made by the Planning Committee involved the proposed audience and the preconference goals. Obviously, these decisions had to be made before the speakers were chosen with the topics they were to cover. Consensus was immediately achieved regarding the audience, namely professionals, paraprofessionals, and library school students involved with or interested in cataloging, public service, or collection development aspects of conference proceedings. From the beginning, the preconference was planned as a unique vehicle to bring all constituencies interested in conference proceedings together to discuss their individual or jointly held concerns. As a result, the following goals were adopted:

> 1) Improve the mechanisms by which user groups access and catalog conference proceedings by increasing the:
> a) understanding of the issues regarding bibliographic control of conference proceedings;
> b) understanding of the application of the current standards for the biblio graphic control of conference proceedings;
> c) awareness of citation practices and their implications for reference and interlibrary loan; and,
> d) understanding of collection development issues related to the acquiring of conference proceedings.
> 2) Make recommendations, as appropriate, regarding bibliographic control and access to conference proceedings.

The Planning Committee discussed a number of potential speakers and, after considerable deliberation, selected the following individuals, who would represent cataloging, public services, collection development, publishers, and a commercial company involved with access to and distribution of published conference materials:

> Moderator: Olivia M.A. Madison (Iowa State University)
> Cataloging: Beacher Wiggins (Library of Congress) and Mary Page (Rutgers University)
> Reference/Interlibrary Loan (public services): Loren Mendelsohn (City College of New York), co-author, and James Ruffner (Wayne State University), co-author
> Collection Development/Publishers (panel discussion): H. Robert Malinowsky (University of Illinois at Chicago), Karen Baschkin (InterDok Corporation), and Jonathan Dahl (IEEE)

In addition to the formal papers and panel discussion, the Planning Committee decided to have practical application (or break-out) sessions that would cover cataloging, reference and interlibrary loan, and collection development and publishing. In order to provide the necessary materials for such sessions, a subgroup of the Planning Committee compiled a workbook that consisted of a variety of examples exploring the different areas of participant interests, a summary of the Library of Congress Rule Interpretations related to the cataloging of conference proceedings, a copy of the ACRL STS recommendations to the publishers of conference proceedings, and a list of the preconference participants. Sara Shatford Layne worked with David Mill and Colby Mariva Riggs to create the camera-ready copy and, using examples gathered by the committee members and some of the speakers, formulated the resulting fourteen "problems." Some of the examples represented problems for catalogers and others for reference librarians and collection development librarians. Samples of title pages, bibliographical records, and actual citations were used to illustrate the problems. The exercises and examples, as well as the discussion leaders' guide, from the workbook are included as Appendixes C and D respectively in this volume.

Finally, the Planning Committee was highly successful in finding corporate sponsors for the preconference. They represented a cross-section of the corporate interests in access (bibliographic and physical) to conference materials and included the following corporations: Engineering Information, Institute for Scientific Information, Kluwer Academic Publishers, OCLC Online Computer Library Center, Inc., and Springer Verlag.

The Preconference

The Preconference on the Bibliographic Control of Conference Proceedings was held on Friday, June 24, 1994, at the Hotel Intercontinental, Miami, Florida from 8:00 am to 4:30 pm. (scheduled before the opening of the American Library Association Annual Conference). The main goal of this preconference was to bring all constituencies interested in conference proceedings together. It was gratifying to all Planning Committee members to see how successfully this goal was met. Indeed, this concept was reiterated by several of the speakers as a way to begin to solve the difficulties related to conference proceedings. In preparation to writing his paper, Beacher Wiggins sought advice at the Library of Congress from catalogers in the Arts and Sciences cataloging Division, staff in the Serials Records Division, and reference librarians in the Science and Technology Division. Likewise, Mary Page described the same sort of process used at Rutgers University when science librarians explored changing the way conference proceedings are cataloged. Jonathan Dahl, to the great enthusiasm of all participants, reported that IEEE had established an advisory committee to recommend standards that it will require its many section conference program paper editors to use when creating title pages, covers, spines, etc. The collection development and reference speakers also mentioned problems with the way indexing and abstracting agencies cite conference proceedings as a contributing factor to the difficulties of locating and obtaining conference proceedings. They also expressed strong interest in merging the best of both cataloging formats (collective classification—serial or set—along with monographic description and access).

The preconference consisted of four parts: three formal papers, a panel discussion including three formal presentations, breakout sessions, and a concluding discussion on possible recommendations from the participants and speakers. As hoped, there were participants representing not only the cataloging area, but also the public services and collection development areas. Three breakout sessions were actually held: two for cataloging (leaders: Beacher Wiggins, Mary Page, and Joan Lussky) and one for public services and collection development (leader: H. Robert Malinowsky).

Perhaps the potentially most far-reaching aspect of the preconference was the set of recommendations that the participants and speakers made to the Planning Committee during the concluding discussion. These recommendations were based on the conference papers and practical applications, and the Planning Committee co-chairs included them in their formal report to ACRL and ALCTS. They are as follows:

1) United States cataloging standards for conference proceedings should be reviewed.

   a) Encourage the Library of Congress to make known its willingness to review its Rule Interpretations, and that it is open to receive recommendations in this vein from outside groups.

   b) Encourage the Library of Congress and CC:DA to review AACR 2 provisions regarding the description and access to conference proceedings with the possible result being rule revision proposals.

   c) Within any such reviews, recommend that input be obtained from the cataloging, public services, and collection development communities.

2) ACRL STS, with input from CC:DA, should consider revising the ACRL STS recommendations for the publishers of conference proceedings so that they will include provisions for electronic conference proceedings.

3) Recommend that ALCTS and ACRL support the efforts of ACRL STS towards turning the ACRL STS recommendations for the publishers of conference proceedings into a national/international standard.

4) Recommend that ALCTS and ACRL reaffirm the ANSI standard for formulation of citations and publicly encourage its usage by indexing and abstracting companies.

The general purposes of these recommendations are to pressure the publishing community to apply more consistency in the presentation of titles and conference names and to provide the best possible bibliographic access to a valuable and complicated literature.

Contributed Papers

This volume contains five of the six papers delivered at the Preconference on the Bibliographic Control of Conference Proceedings. These papers represent the interests of the cataloging, reference/interlibrary loan, and collection development areas, as well as a prominent commercial corporation, InterDok, which has a long history in providing bibliographic and physical access to conference proceedings. Unfortunately Mr. Jonathan Dahl, a speaker at the preconference representing an important publisher of conference materials, Institute of Electrical and Electronics Engineers, was not able to provide the editors with a formal paper representing his presentation. However, the editors have provided a brief abstract of his presentation as part of the following abstracts of the other five papers.

The editors have imposed a certain measure of terminological consistency on the papers included in this volume. We decided to use "name" to refer to what a conference is called (and to what would normally appear in a 1XX or 7XX field of a MARC record) and "title" to refer to what the proceedings of that conference are called (and to what would appear in field 245 subfield ‡a of a MARC record), although this has meant changing the usage of some of the authors. We believe it is important to distinguish between the two concepts by using different words to describe them.

This volume opens with the preconference's keynote paper, "Bibliographic Control of Conference Proceedings" by Beacher Wiggins, in which he begins by providing a succinct and fascinating history of the cataloging treatment of conference proceedings, going as far back as the 1908 *Catalog Rules*. Wiggins thoroughly describes the current cataloging rules, noting the unique treatment AACR 2 calls for when determining main entry, and then briefly discusses the numerous LCRIs that cover conference proceedings, in particular the difficult issues relating to the conference name. He continues by addressing the pivotal description and collocation issue—whether or not this type of material (e.g., proceedings, transactions, abstracts, reports, etc.) should receive serial or monographic treatment. This issue will reoccur in the following four papers, as it often is the crux of the access issue. Wiggins concludes with the offer that LC is willing to review its policies regarding cataloging treatment and entry, with a possible shift towards greater flexibility in deciding how items might be described and how they might be related to previous or later items. Such discussions could result in new LCRIs or rule revision proposals to the Joint Steering Committee for Revision of AACR.

Mary Page, in her paper "Access to Conference Proceedings in a Science Research Library: A Local Perspective," describes how Rutgers University public service science librarians and technical services science librarians came together to discuss the myriad problems of access and collocation resulting from meeting national standards and what decisions evolved out of those discussions. This paper not only represents how one library came to terms with these difficult issues (in particular the issue involving serial versus monographic treatment), but it also provides an excellent methodology as to how public services, collection development, and technical services staff may work together to solve common problems.

Loren Mendelsohn and James A. Ruffner represent reference/interlibrary concerns in their paper "Problems with Conference Proceedings: A Public Services Perspective." They begin discussing these problems by describing why library patrons require assistance in locating conference literature and the numerous tools that patrons and reference librarians should use to verify citations, particularly science-related citations. Mendelsohn and Ruffner briefly discuss the verification and access problems related to the significant portion of conference papers found in the grey literature of science and technology. Then they address the many problems associated with republished or simultaneously published proceedings and provide an interesting discussion involving the citation difficulties associated with conference paper bibliographies. The authors also call for the fullest description and access points possible within bibliographic records and the need for analytical treatment when proceedings are received as regular or special issues of journals. The paper concludes with compelling statistical data to support the case that an increasing percentage of published journal issues consists of conference literature.

The preconference's panel discussion included three speakers representing collection development, a commercial vendor, and a commercial publisher. Following the abstracts of the two published papers is a brief abstract of the panel presentation given by Jonathan Dahl, the marketing director for IEEE.

H. Robert Malinowsky, a collection development officer, opens this section with his paper "Why Collect Conference Proceedings" and makes a serious case for why research libraries should collect this material. In doing so, however, he acknowledges that librarians also must make difficult decisions not to acquire them, often for budgetary reasons. Furthermore, he states that in the sciences, currency is of highest importance, and when that is not possible—whether for publishing, acquiring or cataloging reasons—a collection development officer reluctantly may decide not to acquire them. Malinowsky goes on to deplore the lack of consistency and accuracy in the ways publishers describe these materials in their catalogs and advertisements, often resulting in duplication of materials. He concludes with a call for strict publication standards and a request for the fullest bibliographic descriptions and access points possible, with a clear preference for monographic cataloging treatment (whether as separates or as analytics).

Providing a differing perspective but with some of the same conclusions, Karen Baschkin describes in "Conference Name?: Problems in Identifying and Obtaining Conference Publications" the difficulties a commercial company that specializes in providing verification and distribution services has with identifying and acquiring published conference materials. She also includes an interesting description of InterDok Corporation and its many useful published directories. Baschkin provides a number of lively case studies within her paper that illustrate the communication and access problems associated with sponsoring organizations and their regional groups, publishers with more than one office, changing of sponsoring bodies, and the many ways that the same proceedings may be published. She concludes by giving the general steps to use in researching hard-to-find conference material.

Jonathan Dahl, in his paper given from the perspective of IEEE, concluded the panel by providing an interesting and informative glimpse into the organization of IEEE and raised the hopes of the preconference attendees with the IEEE plan to attempt standardization of the formal presentation of information on conference publications. He began by stating that the annual number of IEEE conferences given in the United States is decreasing; however, the number of IEEE conferences given abroad is increasing, particularly in Eastern Europe and Japan. There are approximately two hundred conferences given each year, and one-fourth of them are held outside the United States. The IEEE organization is akin to the United States federal government and its relationship to the individual states. There is the "federal" organization or office and there are thirty-seven "state–like" technical (e.g., computer) societies or sections, informally staffed by volunteer engineers. Each society or section is managed by individual engineers, and these managers change each year, with little or no continuity. The individual societies and sections make the decisions to hold conferences, have joint societal conferences, select speakers, make local arrangements, etc. The local editor responsible for the resulting publication(s) changes as frequently as the section leadership. The continual change in the local editorial leadership positions is a contributing factor to the many differences in the formatting of information in each publication. However, there is some ray of hope. At the federal level, IEEE has appointed an advisory committee of expert consultants to provide strict guidance to their local editors as to formatting of information, ensuring that the name of the conference and the title of the publication remain the same regardless of location on the publication (e.g., cover title, spine title, running title, etc.). One of the committee members is a member of ACRL STS and a member of this Preconference Planning Committee, Nirmala Bangalore, University of Illinois at Chicago. While Mr. Dahl did not expect that there would be universal adherence to the publication guidelines, he did stress that IEEE is making its best effort to minimize differences in the presentation of information within its publications.

Appendixes

In addition to the papers presented at the conference, this volume contains four appendixes. The material in these appendixes was given to participants at the preconference. Appendix A, prepared by Daniel Kinney, provides a concise history and summary of the Library of Congress Rule Interpretations (issued between 1981 and 1993) that are relevant to conference proceedings. Appendix B is the "Recommendations for Publishers of Conference Proceedings" referred to above. Appendix C consists of exercises/examples prepared for the breakout sessions at the preconference. These exercises and examples are designed to show the problems of conference proceedings from the perspective of public services as well as from technical services. Appendix D is the discussion leaders' guide for the breakout sessions, which was distributed to participants at the close of the preconference.

Concluding remarks

While replete with difficulties involving all aspects of identification, cataloging, and physical accessibility, conference proceedings remain a crucial part of the scientific literature, particularly because of the potential currency of their information and data contained in them. Their importance to research literature is the reason that we have all tried to cope with their enormous difficulties and high costs. Libraries, publishers, indexing and abstracting agencies, and commercial document delivery agencies are the major stakeholders in this crucial segment of research literature, particularly the literature linked to science and technology. Indeed, the highest escalating part of any library's acquisitions budget, the journal acquisitions budget, is a growing repository of this literature and, as a result, is giving libraries little choice in their acquisition and is compounding current bibliographic control problems. Researchers, collection development librarians, and public services librarians all are calling for full cataloging for each individual conference publication, whether as a separate monograph or as an analytic. Or, another costly alternative (as proposed by Page) is to purchase the material twice (both as part of a journal subscription and as a monographic separate) and to give pure monographic treatment to the "separates." Coupled with these costs is the call for the fullest possible descriptive cataloging and access points (with the related authority control) to solve the ridiculously inconsistent and byzantine ways that conference names and published titles are often presented, as well as the inherent difficulties in applying current cataloging rules as to main entry.

The 1994 Preconference on the Bibliographic Control of Conference Proceedings was the first attempt to bring all stakeholders together to identify and possibly agree upon methods that we might all pursue to ease the enormous difficulties that we all face in obtaining, processing, and providing bibliographic and physical access to this vital literature. Clearly all stakeholders must collectively solve the complex problems associated with conference proceedings. The six speakers described many potential solutions, including methods of bringing local and national stakeholders together to identify and decide upon solutions, mechanisms for coping with current verification difficulties and publishing patterns, the possibility of reviewing the current cataloging code and LCRIs to simplify (we hope) the cataloging process by recognizing some of the unique circumstances related to conference materials, and increasing the national level of analytical cataloging for those proceedings issued as part of journals. The examples and exercises used within the workshop and found in Appendix C not only provide good training materials but also demonstrate the need for solutions to the bibliographic quagmire into which this literature has sunk.

The recommendations that evolved out of this workshop could help resolve many of the difficulties addressed in the six papers and assist in lowering—or at least maintaining—their costs, both in terms of personnel and materials. Their acceptance would result in publishers using standard guidelines for portraying conference names and titles, abstracting and indexing agencies following current ANSI standards for formulating citations, and the cataloging community re-evaluating their descriptive and access rules and standards in light of the current difficulties in application.

Bibliographic Control of Conference Proceedings

Beacher Wiggins

When Olivia Madison called me last year to see if I would take part in this preconference, I was delighted to say yes. She went on to explain that I was being asked to present an overview of current national policies, standards, and issues associated with bibliographic control of conference proceedings. I still said yes. After we hung up, it struck me what I had agreed to do. What a daunting task! When I sought the approval of my boss, Sarah Thomas, the Director for Cataloging at the Library of Congress, to participate, I forwarded to her a copy of Olivia's letter and draft program outline. She granted approval but also added the reply, "Beacher, I'm glad you'll be speaking, but what a topic!" The more I explored and contemplated it, the more I became convinced of the complexity and immensity involved in bringing conference proceedings under bibliographic control.

Robert Oseman neatly summed up the challenge when he stated:

Titles, themes, eye-catching buzz-words of thematic significance, . . . sponsors, co-sponsors, dates, both of the event and the proceedings, and the frequent absence of any of these elements form a melting-pot of uncertainty, from which has to be drawn meaningful cataloguing data and subject classification.[1]

Add to this cauldron the fact that conference proceedings can be issued regularly (often making them serial in nature) or irregularly, that they can be published as monographs, as special issues of serials, and as part of a monographic series. All of these possibilities help to confound an easy resolution to how such publications should be treated. Additionally, title page layouts are often unclear, exacerbating the confusion. Finally, how should these items be entered—under conference name or title?

1

But even with the knowledge of what one would be facing, it seemed appropriate that someone from LC should be participating in this gathering, as much for what we can gain from as for what we can contribute to the discussions. As the chief of the Arts and Sciences Cataloging Division, where a large percentage of such publications is processed at LC, I was willing to take a stab at the task. I also must confess to what some may view as a perverse sort of pleasure—when I was still an active cataloger, conference proceedings (and Bibles) were always favorite items to catalog!

Historical Treatment of Conference Publications

Where to begin? I thought I would start by reviewing the treatment of conference publications in our national cataloging rules during this century. In taking a historical detour to see how we got to where we are currently with respect to the cataloging of conference proceedings, I would like to begin by quoting one of the chief architects of our cataloging canon, Charles A. Cutter, who in the fourth edition of his *Rules for a Dictionary Catalog*, lamented:

> Still I cannot help thinking that the golden age of cataloging is over, and that the difficulties and discussions which have furnished an innocent pleasure to so many will interest them no more.[2]

While some might argue that the golden age of cataloging is indeed over, today's Preconference is testimony to the ongoing difficulties associated with cataloging one category of material. It further corroborates that there is more at stake than mere innocent pleasure on the parts of those engaged in essaying to bring control to this material that is used so heavily by so many people, but that presents a plethora of problems in the bargain. Sorting through the complexities is the challenge before us. By the end of my talk, I may have recited more problems and questions than answers. The answers may need to come from other sources, maybe some of you or our colleagues in the library community, with LC playing a role.

I went back as far as the 1908 *Catalog Rules: Author and Title Entries* in tracing the treatment accorded conference proceedings. In that code, conferences were set off in a special group of rules that included

> conferences, congresses, exhibitions, and other occasional meetings, firms and other business concerns, committees and classes of citizens not belonging to any body or organization, ecclesiastical councils, foundations and endowments, expeditions, etc.[3]

There were separate rules for diplomatic congresses, international meetings, exhibitions, etc., conventions, conferences, and committees and meetings of citizens. Of particular interest is the instruction in rule 105 of that code to

> enter conventions and conferences of bodies which have no existence beyond the convention under the name of the convention. If no name can be found, enter under the place of meeting and supply a name descriptive of the character of the convention.[4]

Moving to the 1949 *A.L.A. Cataloging Rules for Author and Title Entries,* we find that they expanded considerably the guidance offered in processing conference publications. In addition to more detailed instruction being included under the categories cited in the 1908 *Rules,* rules for the following were listed in the 1949 code: congresses of groups of states having similar language and culture, national congresses, institutes, conferences, conventions, etc. Again, catalogers were told that "if no name can be found for the meeting, enter it under the place and supply a name descriptive of the character of the meeting."[5]

The first edition of the *Anglo-American Cataloging Rules,* published in 1967, continued the trend set by its immediate predecessor in the expansive instructions it supplied. For the first time, separate rules were devoted to the additions to include in the heading for a named meeting. An explicit statement on what constitutes, or rather (in this case) what does not constitute, a name, is worth pointing out because of the difficulty this concept causes in the current rules.

> A meeting of the general membership of an organization that is simply called 'Conference (Convention, etc.) of the (organization)' is considered to be an activity of the body as a whole and without corporate character of its own.[6]

Under this condition, the notion of a generic conference name is ignored and main entry becomes the corporate body.

With this brief historical foray, we come to our current code, the second edition of the *Anglo-American Cataloguing Rules,* first issued in 1978 and subsequently updated in a 1988 revision, commonly called AACR 2.

The Current Cataloging Rules

I will begin our look at AACR 2 by quoting one of its editors, Michael Gorman:

> The rules in chapter 24 provide examples of the treatment of the names of bodies such as conferences and exhibitions (already admitted as corporate bodies in chapter 21), which will help in the solution of this *minor* [italics added] but difficult problem.[7]

One is struck by the end of Mr. Gorman's statement and could easily wonder which adjective carries the day, "minor" or "difficult"—was he alluding to the "minor" nature of conferences as corporate bodies or to the "difficult" level they represent as material to catalog. Rather than questioning his meaning, it is more instructive to turn to AACR 2 to see what guidance it offers, since our national policy is derived from its rules. Rule 21.1B covers when to enter under a corporate body. That rule also gives the definition of both a corporate body and a particular type of corporate body, a conference.

> A corporate body is an organization or a group of persons that is identified by a particular name and that acts, or may act, as an entity.[8]

> Conferences are meetings of individuals or representatives of various bodies for the purpose of discussing and/or acting on topics of common interest, or meetings of representatives of a corporate body that constitute its legislative or governing body.[9]

Rule 21.1B2 is the general rule that specifies which works may be entered under a corporate body. First, a work must emanate from a corporate body, which means that "it is issued by that body or has been caused to be issued by that body or . . . originated with that body."[10] Category d of the rule addresses conferences. This category encompasses

> those that report the collective activity of a conference (e.g., proceedings, collected papers), . . . falling within the definition of a corporate body . . ., provided that the conference . . . is prominently named . . . in the item being catalogued.[11]

It is curious that among corporate bodies, only conferences are singled out in the restriction to being used in the main entry only if they appear prominently (i.e., on the title page, other preliminaries—verso of title page, any pages preceding the title page, cover—and colophon). I'll return to this point later.

Having decided on the entry of a conference publication, one next seeks guidance on how to formulate the heading by turning to chapter 24. Rule 24.1A speaks to constructing corporate bodies in general, citing several conference names among the examples. For information on how to handle certain variant presentations of conference names, rule 24.3F offers solutions for choosing a name when two conditions exist: 1) a conference name includes the name of a corporate body associated with the meeting and 2) a conference has both a specific and a general name. Conference names get their own rule (24.7, Conferences, Congresses, Meetings, Etc.) under the general rubric "Additions, Omissions, and Modifications," where omissions and additions (number, date, location) are spelled out. Although the concept was present by example in earlier cataloging codes, AACR 2 introduced an additional complexity for conference headings by prescribing that a conference is to be considered named when it is subordinate to another corporate entity. Rules 24.13A, type 3 ("a name that is general in nature or that does no more than indicate a geographic, chronological, or numbered or lettered subdivision of a parent body") and type 6 ("a name that includes the entire name of the higher or related body") elucidate this idea, with the examples listed of meetings entered subordinately to a corporate entity.

This synopsis of the present rules sets the stage for us to examine how the rules are interpreted. Of course, interpretation of the rules is a role the Library of Congress has assumed for years now. Our interpretations are shared with the library community in the published Library of Congress Rule Interpretations as well as part of *Cataloging Service Bulletin.* An excellent "Chronology and Summary" of the LCRIs relating to conference proceedings has been prepared by Daniel Kinney, one of the Preconference organizers, and included as part of the workbook each of you received. [Editors' note: this "Chronology and Summary" appears as Appendix A in this volume.] One measure of the difficulties attendant to conference publications is the number of changes to the LCRIs that has been issued since the adoption of AACR 2 in 1981—a fact that Daniel has underscored in his chronology.

The Cataloging Policy and Support Office, under the administrative authority of the Director for Cataloging, is the unit at LC responsible for setting cataloging policy for LC's catalogers, and by extension, the nation's catalogers as well. In preparing for this presentation, I necessarily met with the descriptive cataloging policy specialists in that Office who deal most frequently with queries and problems stemming from cataloging conference publications. They were all sympathetic to the topic and the need to focus attention on it. Each specialist had his or her view of the issues that abound and each could offer anecdotes and questions that had been raised over the course of years that pertained directly to cataloging conference proceedings. The specialists always advise those who consult them to start with the rules (AACR 2) for guidance, but they quickly point out that when the rules are relied on solely, the rules are found wanting in several respects. This deficiency has accounted for the number of LCRIs that has been generated since the appearance of AACR 2. Each iteration of these LCRIs was the result of LC's endeavoring to address perceived flaws or gaps in the rules, to fill in where the rules were silent, and to articulate a national policy that could be used more easily by all catalogers. Even with the issuance of LCRIs to assist with application of the rules, there remain imprecise direction and conflicting implications for handling certain situations relative to conferences. Are more rule interpretations the answer or is now a propitious time to contemplate revision to the rules themselves?

What's in a Name?

A conference by any other name is equally sweet (or, more likely, equally problematic): congress, symposium, colloquium, seminar, meeting, institute, workshop, convention, assembly, school—and these are just some common English language equivalents. Then there are the initialisms and other non-conventional brief names. Determining what is a named conference is often less than a simple exercise. Many questions arise: Must there be a definite article preceding the name? Does the use of an indefinite article negate the status of the phrase as being named? Is the absence of a word denoting a meeting indication that there is no name involved? Because proceedings of conferences lacking the presence of a conference name are in essence treated as anonymous works and thereby given title main entry by default, what is named and what is unnamed become of utmost importance. In 1975, Eva Verona registered her surprise at the virtually total lack of attention paid in the pre-Paris Principles (1961) literature to the issue of what is a named conference. She went on to note that the void had not been adequately filled in the intervening years to 1975, not even by AACR 1, whose definition of a conference she characterized as vague.[12] In 1994, although a restructured and thoroughly reworked code (AACR 2) has appeared, we are still grappling with this thorny aspect of cataloging conference publications, e.g., what is a name. But, providing that a name can be ascertained, Verona, after comparing the use of conference headings in library catalogs and national bibliographies, concluded that "author entry for named conferences remains the best solution, provided simple and straightforward rules are established and followed."[13]

The LC policy specialists pretty much agreed that LCRI 21.1B1, which provides guidance on what constitutes a name, needs rewriting because it is proving inadequate in embracing the very large number of conference names that appears in abbreviated form, e.g., **COMSAC '92**, **Eurotrib 81**, **IECON '93**, etc. There is little guidance on how to determine that such a term constitutes a name, short of the example that is cited by exception—**Darmstadter Gesprach**. It has now become the general policy that the appearance of the year as an integral part of the term is sufficient documentation to support the conference's being named. The rule interpretation further allows for establishing an increasing number of headings for meetings that can be argued not truly to be named. Some feel that names are being ascribed to meetings that are merely general descriptions rather than specific appellations, as called for in the definition for a corporate body in AACR 2, rule 21.1B1—this same definition that Eva Verona finds nettlesome. The presence of the term for the gathering, e.g., "symposium" in **UCLA Symposium**, in conjunction with the name or abbreviation of a corporate body is deemed sufficient to strengthen a weak phrase so that it is a named conference. Are such constructions serving a useful function? By establishing a pattern of treating these occurrences as headings, are users being trained to seek publications under these names (which may prove useful in the long term)?

LCRI 21.1B1 resulted from the Library's attempt to respond to the many questions it had received centering on these types of conference names following adoption of AACR 2. A huge percentage was owing to the change ushered in by the code that stipulated that generic terms are considered to be named meetings. The circumstances are not always clear and the distinctions between meetings of a body versus meetings only sponsored by a body are often blurred.

In an article published in 1990, Dorothy McGarry and Martha Yee have presented a cogent and eloquent assessment of the morass engendered by this aspect of the rules for conference headings.[14] They stop somewhat short of recommending solutions, although they do offer up some conclusions based on a survey they sent to head reference librarians at 363 libraries. The authors' aims were to determine if reference librarians in large libraries have a tendency to search for proceedings associated with the name of the holding body and a generic meeting term under this combination—where the current LCRIs would place them, and if there is a distinct choice among reference librarians for any of the four ways the authors posed for assigning main entry for this class of conference name. Their four methods for entry were 1) direct entry, e.g., **Convention of the Alliance of Concerned Artists**; 2) subordinate entry, e.g., **Alliance of Concerned Artists. Convention**; 3) entry under holding body, e.g., **Alliance of Concerned Artists**; and 4) entry under title, e.g., **Proceedings of the first Convention of the Alliance of Concerned Artists**. Their conclusions were that 1) there is a clear preference for giving main entry to the corporate body holding the meeting for the type of conference proceedings under discussion here; and 2) present practice, however, of entry of the generic conference name as a subordinate element of the corporate body seems to be useful as long as main entry under the name of the corporate body alone is prohibited.

A clarification of LC's position on how to handle these situations was offered to the library community in the spring 1985 number of *Cataloging Service Bulletin*. A summary of that clarification remains the policy today, although some at the Library feel that further work is needed in this area to respond to some of the questions posited above. This current policy can be summarized as follows:

1) Consider any combination of corporate name and meeting designation to be named;

2) Consider the appearance of a generic name alone, in the case of a meeting *of a corporate body*, to be named;

3) Consider the appearance of a generic name alone, in the case of a meeting *only sponsored by a corporate body*, to be unnamed;

4) If the generic meeting is determined to be named, enter it subordinately to the corporate body whether it appears alone or in conjunction with the name of the corporate body;

5) Enter all other named meetings, e.g., those that contain subject words, or that are abbreviations or other brief forms, directly under their own names.

It might also be useful here to summarize the LC policy for access points on conference publications.

1) Main entry is under a named conference only if that name is presented in the chief source of information; otherwise, entry is under title. The Library made this change because of problems presented by the fluid state of title pages and preliminaries in prepublication galleys received to be cataloged as part of the Cataloging-in-Publication Program.

2) An added entry is given to a named conference that appears anywhere in the item, if it was not given main entry because it did not appear on the chief source of information.

3) An added entry is given to a corporate body that sponsors a meeting only if it is named prominently in the item.

Before moving from this aspect of our topic, another problem associated with subordinate entry of generic conference names should be highlighted, namely, one having to do with the MARC coding: Even though the formats are logical in their prescription, it is very difficult for some catalogers to accept that a subordinate conference name is coded as a field X10 subfield ‡b, rather than a field X11.

Is It a Serial or Monograph?

Proceedings, transactions, abstracts, papers, report, record—these are among the common English language titles encountered on publications emanating from conferences. These are just the type of titles that cry out for treatment as a serial. Once a decision is made about how to enter conference proceedings, probably the next question is whether to catalog the publication as a serial or monograph. There is much about such publications that would commend them to serial processing. They share several similarities with serials and are mentioned in the definition in AACR 2 for a serial:

> a publication in any medium issued in successive parts bearing numeric or chronological designations and intended to be continued indefinitely. Serials include . . . the journals, memoirs, proceedings, transactions, etc., of societies . . .[15]

In addition to possessing generic titles, conference proceedings, like serials, are collections of articles; conference proceedings appear regularly; and conference proceedings may announce particulars about future conferences. The argument on which way to handle them is circular, with ready evidence to support both types of treatment. Michael Unsworth asserts that, "from a purely technical processing standpoint, cataloging conference publications as serials can be very attractive."[16] It is easier to treat an incoming item as an added piece to a serial (handled by a paraprofessional) than it is to treat it as a monograph and be required to create a new record (handled by a cataloger). Additionally, the very real benefit to be gained from having all the volumes shelve together is a decided advantage. Of course, stability in presentation—of the name of the conference, of the title, of the numbering designation—from piece to piece must prevail to make serial treatment practicable.

It must be conceded that some access is lost if serial cataloging is chosen. While acknowledging this loss of access, Unsworth goes on to argue that "thematic titles, editors, occasional sponsoring bodies, subject headings, and individual classification (the main virtues of monographic cataloging) are often of minor concern."[17] In describing how Columbia University accords serial cataloging to conference proceedings, Michael

Borries aligns with Unsworth by questioning the usefulness of access points for sponsors, editors, and theme titles.[18] Jim Cole, on the other hand, counters that "the various problems attendant upon cataloging conference publications as serials lead one to conclude that the monographic approach is undoubtedly better."[19] He further asks "whether conference publications can form a serial, or whether the conferences themselves merely form a series."[20] This poses an interesting question and lends credence to a suggestion espoused by some that, in dealing with conference publications, we should catalog the event rather than an artifact of the event, i.e., the publication. In such a case, the event is treated as serial and the publications of the event are collected under a "uniform title."

Consultations with reference librarians in LC's Science and Technology Division, where many conference publications are serviced to the public, yielded a consensus that, on balance, processing conference proceedings as serials generally serves the best interests of patrons. The staff's experience at the reference desk has shown them that a search for a title sought by a patron should begin in the serials database. If the volumes have been cataloged as a serial, the staff have the comfort of knowing that all the pieces will be classed together. They further recognized that as serials, the pieces generally progressed through the processing stream faster, ultimately becoming available to users more speedily. Their nod was to serial treatment.

A shift towards more flexibility in deciding when an item can be handled as a serial is one worth pursuing. Discussions with colleagues in the Serial Record Division, the unit at LC responsible for cataloging serials, revealed that there is receptiveness to such a shift. The Library has eased the situation of title changes of serials by expanding the number and types of variations permitted that are not to be judged a new serial entry, making LCRI 21.2A and 21.2C less restrictive now than in past years. But, as currently applied, LCRI 12.0A remains constraining in the latitude allowed for applying serial techniques in the first instance of cataloging. Greater service might be rendered if catalogers were permitted to exercise judgment in deciding how soon in the sequence of publications—even as early as the first instance—the item can be called a serial. Currently, based on the latest issuance of the LCRI, we use an unstated rule of thumb of three publications with stable presentations of data before making them a serial. In fact, the Library's National Serials Data Program issues ISSNs on request to publishers for the first appearance of a conference volume without the documented evidence that subsequent volumes will display seriality. Yes, by taking a more liberal approach, there are surely to be cases when inappropriate decisions will be made and the next piece received will have a different title requiring that a different serial entry be created; but, in the long run, greater stability in treatment would occur by adopting the more lax approach. To take care of situations where it is desirable at the local level not to follow national practice if we make this kind of transition (as well as for current conference proceedings cataloged as serials), brief (or full, if warranted) records could be created for any subsequent pieces that may have special or theme titles worthy of analysis.

If this departure is not palatable, another change might be contemplated: within the current *LCRI*, the instruction to "catalog earlier and later title changes" as serials could be amended to rescind the current mandate to recatalog the existing monograph records. A note indicating the existence of other volumes cataloged as monographs ought to suffice. Further, once a conference publication has been dealt with as a serial, the conditions under which it would be viewed as having changed significantly enough to require a new serial entry should be restricted. The MARC format provides for relational connections using the linking entry fields (the 76X-78X fields). And, as I understand it, after format integration is implemented, the capability will be extended to link serial and monograph records.

I caution here that these are the thoughts of a non-serials cataloger, buttressed by discussions with serials catalogers, and certainly bear further investigation by those better positioned to reach sound decisions. But there was interest on the parts of my Serial Record Division colleagues in exploring a change in approach. In fact, during this Annual Conference, one of them will informally confer with CONSER participants to see if there is similar interest on the part of those in the CONSER community. If so, an informal group may flesh out some of these ideas for presentation at the CONSER meeting scheduled for this coming November at LC.

Subject Cataloging and Shelflisting of Conference Publications
The Library disseminates guidance on subject cataloging and shelflisting of conference proceedings via the *Subject Cataloging Manual: Subject Headings* (section H 1460, Congresses); *Subject Cataloging Manual: Classification* (section F 240, Congresses); and *Subject Cataloging Manual: Shelflisting* (section G 230, Conferences, Congresses, Meetings, Etc.). I have not, however, devoted any time to these aspects of cataloging conference proceedings. Based on my discussions with subject cataloging policy specialists in LC's Policy Office and reference staff at LC, most of the complications central to conference proceedings derive from the elements of description and entry, including determining when a conference is named and how that name is to be constructed. The one point that was a common thread in discussions with reference librarians and in the literature related to the need to have conference proceedings classified together—a concern alluded to earlier and one that the recommendation to process more proceedings as serials would help to ensure.

The Library's policy for cuttering items with a conference main entry is to include in the cutter number the date in the conference heading and not the publication date. This represents one component of the national policy: the National Library of Medicine made a decision several years ago that is at variance with this policy. The National Library of Medicine now uses the date of publication as part of the cutter. Its decision to change its practice was based on the several changes in instructions in the LCRIs (which reasons have previously been explained) on when the conference name could be given as main entry. For title main entries, the date of publication is used in the cutter number by both national institutions.

Next Steps
Where do we go from here? I am hopeful that some recommendations will be forthcoming from the interchange that will occur here today while we have cataloging, reference, and collections development librarians, along with publishers, convened in one setting. The Library of Congress is open to receiving recommendations in this vein from outside groups. If there is a group in the library community interested in pursuing some of the issues raised today, with an aim towards assisting LC in revising the pertinent LCRIs, that would be welcomed. Further, if some of those recommendations would suggest themselves as possible candidates for rule revision, that avenue may be open as well, since LC has a representative to the Joint Steering Committee for Revision of AACR. A prime question for possible consideration for rule revision is why, in rule 21.1B2, category d ("those that report the collective activity of a conference") is the sole category requiring that, in order to get main entry, the corporate body (the conference) must be presented

prominently in the item being cataloged. In light of the evidence that seekers of these publications often ask for them by elements of the conference name, oblivious to whether the conference name has appeared prominently on the item sought, prominence seems less persuasive as a requirement. Moreover, there is abundant evidence that citations to the publications cite the conference names, with seemingly scant regard to how or where the conference name appears in the publication.

I have already mentioned that suggestions for rethinking seriality and conference proceedings may be put to the CONSER community, which, in turn, may yield proposals for changes in this area. I think there is promise for movement in regard to processing conference publications and I think we can all be a part of it. I am anxious to hear your reactions as the day progresses.

Notes

1. Robert Oseman. *Conferences and Their Literature: A Question of Value.* (London: Library Association, 1989), p. 38.

2. Charles A. Cutter. *Rules for a Dictionary Catalog*, 4th ed. rewritten. (Washington: Government Printing Office, 1904), p. 5.

3. *Catalog Rules: Author and Title Entries.* Compiled by Committees of the American Library Association and the (British) Library Association. American ed. (Boston: ALA Publishing Board, 1908), p. 30.

4. *Ibid*, 31.

5. *A.L.A. Cataloging Rules for Author and Title Entries.* Prepared by the Division of Cataloging and Classification of the American Library Association. 2nd ed. Edited by Clara Beetle. (Chicago: ALA, 1949), p. 203.

6. *Anglo-American Cataloging Rules.* Prepared by the American Library Association, the Library of Congress, the Library Association, and the Canadian Library Association. North American text. (Chicago: ALA, 1967), p. 133.

7. Michael Gorman. "The *Anglo-American Cataloguing Rules*, Second Edition." *Library Resources & Technical Services* 22:3 (summer 1978), p. 223.

8. *Anglo-American Cataloguing Rules.* Prepared under the direction of the Joint Steering Committee for Revision of AACR. Edited by Michael Gorman and Paul W. Winkler. 2nd ed., 1988 revision. (Chicago: American Library Association, 1988), p. 312.

9. *Ibid*, 313.

10. *Ibid*, 313.

11. *Ibid*, 313.

12. Eva Verona. *Corporate Headings: Their Use in Library Catalogues and National Bibliographies: A Comparative and Critical Study.* (London: IFLA Committee on Cataloguing, 1975), p. 122.

13. *Ibid*, 136.

14. Dorothy McGarry and Martha M. Yee. "Cataloging Conference Proceedings: A Survey and Comments." *Library Resources & Technical Services* 34:1 (January 1990), p. 44-53.

15. *Anglo-American Cataloguing Rules*, 622.

16. Michael E. Unsworth. "Treating IEEE Conference Publications as Serials." *Library Resources & Technical Services* 27:2 (April/June 1983), p. 222.

17. *Ibid*, 222.

18. Michael S. Borries. "Cataloging Conference Publications: Problems and Issues." *Science & Technology Libraries* 9:2 (winter 1988), p. 32.

19. Jim Cole. "Conference Publications: Serials or Monographs?" *Library Resources & Technical Services* 22:2 (spring 1978), p. 171.

20. *Ibid*, 170.

Access to Conference Proceedings in a Science Research Library: A Local Perspective

Mary Page

When I first heard about this program, I have to admit that there was a part of me that was very relieved. At Rutgers University, we had begun looking at the way proceedings were being cataloged, and I was overwhelmed by the complexities of local processing practices. To learn that there was interest in the bibliographic control of conference proceedings in the larger library community was, in many ways, a validation that the problems we had been grappling with were very real. We were not alone.

I speak as a technical services librarian with a strong public service orientation, or maybe a public services librarian with a strong technical services orientation. I no longer do cataloging myself, but from previous experience as a cataloger at a technical institute, I do have a feel for science cataloging. My primary responsibilities currently fall under the technical services rubric, but I participate in public services as well. At Rutgers, all of the science librarians, including the director, serve at the reference desk. Having a cataloging background has helped me enormously at the reference desk, and I like to think that this first-hand experience with patrons has made me a better technical services librarian.

I think we are all here today for one primary reason: conference proceedings are a major resource in science collections, but they are very difficult to control and manage. A conference that for years has been sponsored by one society suddenly becomes a joint conference with two other organizations. A conference may have a different theme each year or the word order of the title changes slightly. For science libraries, confer-

---

FIGURE 1

Keyword Search on: ACM THEORY COMPUTING

102   RUTGERS UNIVERSITY   -IRIS LIBRARY SYSTEM   ALL *BOOLEAN SEARCH

1.   ACM Symposium on Theory of Computing.

2.   ACM Symposium on Theory of Computing, 7th, Albuquerque, N.M., 1975.

3.   ACM Symposium on Theory of Computing, 8th, Hershey Pa., 1976.

4.   ACM Symposium on Theory of Computing, 9th, Boulder, Colo., 1977.

5.   ACM Symposium on Theory of Computing, 11th, Atlanta, 1979.

6.   ACM Symposium on Theory of Computing (13th : 1981 : Milwaukee, Wis.)

---

ence proceedings present numerous challenges in terms of both public services *and* technical services.

Put simply, the problem at Rutgers was this: the science librarians began noticing that more and more conference proceedings seemed to be cataloged as serials. As an example, in the Rutgers University's IRIS Library System (a Geac system) I did a keyword search on "ACM theory computing" with the following summary search result. Figure 1 is a serial record (with no date), and five monograph records follow representing the individual symposia held from 1975 through 1981. As you can easily tell, these individual symposia records provide the place where the conferences were held (e.g., Albuquerque, Boulder, Atlanta, etc.).

If I select the serial record, figure 2 shows the IRIS display for the symposia from 1982 forward.

Immediately obvious is that there are no conference locations on the serial record. If I were to do a keyword search for "ACM Computing Albuquerque," I would be able to zoom in on the 1975 conference. That kind of search is not possible for the sessions from 1982 forward.

This one example illustrates the impact for OPAC displays and searching when cataloging is changed from monographic to serial treatment. It also illustrates the reason for the formal investigation and a series of discussions among Rutgers public and tech-nical services librarians regarding local cataloging policies for conference proceedings. The experience was illuminating for all of us. What I would like to share with you is the essence of that experience—what we learned and what we decided. And, if you will indulge me, I would like to give a few personal observations.

As background, let me explain how the Rutgers libraries are organized. The Technical and Automated Services Department provides centralized technical services for all sixteen Rutgers libraries. There are six science libraries: the main science library is the Library of Science and Medicine, known as LSM. LSM has five branches: Chemistry, Physics, Mathematics, the Center for Alcohol Studies, and Entomology. An agriculture library is presently under construction. All of the branch libraries are located physically in the departments they serve. In essence, our serials operations are decentralized, while our cataloging and monographic acquisitions operations are centralized.

FIGURE 2

102   RUTGERS UNIVERSITY   -IRIS LIBRARY SYSTEM   ALL *BOOLEAN SEARCH

Citation 1 of 6

AUTHOR ACM Symposium on Theory of Computing.
TITLE   Proceedings of the ... annual ACM Symposium on Theory of Computing.
PUBLISHER New York, N.Y. : Association for Computing Machinery, Inc., 1982-

Location	Loan Type	Call Number	Cpy #	Status
MATH	STACKS	QA76.5.A7 yr.1992	1	In Library
MATH	RES 2	QA76.5.A7 yr.1991	1	On Reserve
MATH	RES 2	QA76.5.A7 yr.1990	1	On Reserve
MATH	RES 2	QA76.5.A7 yr.1989	1	On Reserve
MATH	RES 2	QA76.5.A7 yr.1988	1	On Reserve
MATH	RES 2	QA76.5.A7 yr.1987	1	On Reserve
MATH	RES 2	QA76.5.A7 yr.1986	1	On Reserve

During our discussions on conference proceedings, a separate but related issue arose: how special issues of journals were to be cataloged. As you know, conference proceedings often appear in a special issue of a scientific journal. As a result of these discussions, two task forces composed of technical and public services librarians were formed. One task force was to study and make recommendations for the cataloging treatment of conference proceedings in the sciences. The other task force was to do the same for special issues of journal publications. Because of my role as technical services librarian for the science libraries, I served on both.

Let me outline the different points of view. The science librarians like conference proceedings cataloged as sets with analytics. At Rutgers, we call this treatment "cat/set/a." Each item gets a separate cataloging record with full bibliographic description and its own access points. "Cataloged as a set" means that the conference is classified together. If you will recall the ACM example, before 1982 there was a separate cataloging record for each year of the conference, but they all had the same call number. One advantage of "cat/set/a" treatment is that because they are shelved together, many patrons know where to find "their" conferences in the stacks. You get the physical collocation that comes with serial treatment, but you also get individual access points to editors, locations, and special topics. Truly the best of both worlds.

On the other hand, technical services librarians like to follow Library of Congress treatment and classification whenever possible. Lower-level staff can perform copy cataloging, and the less tinkering they have to do to individual records, the faster materials get processed. And, the less customizing we do to records, the cheaper it is.

There was also another problem, a local one, and it came down to semantics. We all have our own institutional cans of worms, and this was one at Rutgers. "Cat/set/a" treatment at Rutgers is defined as a series treatment. When certain conditions are met, and the MARC tags 4XX and 8XX are involved, copy catalogers consult the manual series authority file. The series authority file gives the authorized series heading and the authorized treatment or classification. If a series at Rutgers is classified under one call number, that decision is recorded in the series authority file.

However, at Rutgers, "cat/set/a" treatment for conference proceedings presented difficulties for the cataloging workflow, because not all conference proceedings are published as a series. The name of a conference is often a main or an added entry, not a series entry. For this reason, conference proceedings are not included in the Rutgers series authority file, which is the source of information for treatment and classification decisions for our catalogers.

We were stretching the definition of series when we referred to conference proceedings as "cat/set/a." It may seem a minor thing, but when you process enormous quantities of materials, as most research libraries do, clear definitions make for smooth operations. Using "cat/set/a" for conferences did not fit the definition. Basically the problem was: how can we tell the copy catalogers to consult the series authority file to find a classification for a conference proceedings? We were talking apples and oranges.

How did we get away with "cat/set/a" treatment for conference proceedings previously? Well, things were different in the good old days. There was a science cataloger who understood the complexities of science materials and who, quite frankly, performed a lot of what we affectionately called "curbside" or custom cataloging for the science libraries. When she retired, we were not able to fill that position, and original cataloging operations were consolidated. With resources in short supply, it became increasingly important to process as much material as possible through copy cataloging.

To begin our study of cataloging treatment for conferences and special issues of journals, we not only searched the literature but also took it to the streets, so to speak, on the various electronic lists on the Internet. Science librarians put out queries on various lists for librarians in engineering, chemistry, physics, and maps, among others. Technical services people queried AUTOCAT, the authorities and cataloging list. While the formal literature search provided good background information, the informal and unofficial feedback from the librarians on the lists really helped define the issues in terms of current practice.

It came as no surprise that, in our informal Internet survey, everyone agreed that conference proceedings are difficult and expensive to catalog and manage. Also, everyone had a horror story. The basic dilemma for everyone seems to be whether to catalog conference proceedings as monographs or as serials. Serial treatment can be more efficient on the cataloging end, but fewer access points are provided. Monographic treatment can be more labor-intensive for catalogers, but more access points are provided. At first glance, this seems to be a cost versus access issue.

We obtained many strong opinions on this topic from our Internet survey. Let me try to summarize the discussion. Advocates of serials treatment pointed out that fewer bibliographic records are involved in serials cataloging, which has the advantage of saving cataloging time and record space in online systems. Also, holdings are collocated both on the shelf and on one bibliographic record, making it easier for patrons to determine what is owned. Another reason given is that indexes and abstracts provide the best analysis of conference proceedings, so why don't we just rely on those commercial services?

More prevalent were the advocates for monographic treatment, who did not believe that serials cataloging for conferences is more efficient and cost-effective. The main reason mentioned was that frequent name and title changes negate any cost-savings in cataloging. Serials catalogers are generally more experienced and therefore paid more, and serials cataloging is generally more complex and time-consuming. Many librarians surveyed on the lists said that it is a misperception that shelving collocation can be

---

FIGURE 3

Serials Treatment for Conference Proceedings

PROS:

1) Fewer bibliographic records; saves on cataloging time and record space.
2) Holdings are shelved together.
3) Subject specific indexes and abstracts already analyze conference proceedings.

CONS:

1) Frequent name and title changes negate any savings on cataloging time.
2) Serials cataloging is (generally) more complex, therefore more time consuming (and more expensive).
3) Savings achieved on the cataloging end are simply passed down the line to public services.

---

achieved only through serials treatment. Indeed, it is not uncommon for librarians to find ways to keep conferences shelved together, sometimes by simply ignoring changes that would result in a change in cuttering.

Another point made by the Rutgers science librarians and reiterated on the lists was this: any savings of time and resources on the cataloging end are passed down the line to public services in the form of more time spent helping patrons find what they need or more interlibrary loan requests being generated for materials that are actually owned by the library. The science librarians indicated that they often log onto several databases (e.g., RLIN, OCLC, and subject-specific indexes) simply to nail down one conference. They pointed to the cost of acquiring material that never gets used because it is inaccessible. There is also the more important and intangible cost to researchers and to the institutions we serve: information that cannot be used.

Figures 3 and 4 provide brief topical outlines of the discussions that took place as the public services and technical services librarians dealt with the issues involving serial and monograph treatments.

There were long and productive discussions, and all of the Rutgers librarians agreed that providing thorough access was important. They also understood the benefits of monographic cataloging—you get access to editors, locations, special themes, co-sponsors. Science librarians cited example after example of researchers approaching the reference desk and asking about "that conference on fractals in Borneo." How can you find something like that unless "Borneo" is searchable? And yes, indexes and abstracts provide access to conferences, but many services index only selectively. Besides, indexing becomes meaningless if you can't find the primary resource. Our online catalogs should *reveal* what we own.

FIGURE 4

Monographic Treatment for Conferences

1) Provides access to individual locations, editors, special themes, co-sponsors, etc.
2) Makes it possible to find "that conference on fractals in Borneo."
3) Indexing and abstracts fully analyze proceedings, but can patrons find them in our online catalog?
4) Online catalogs should reveal, not conceal.

However, the librarians recognized that in this harsh fiscal climate, following LC practice as much as possible makes the best use of our technical services resources. We made some compromises. Public services librarians yielded some on the serials vs. monographs issue, but some important exceptions were agreed upon. Here is what the first task force recommended:

When LC changes a conference from monographic to serials treatment, we would follow LC when these three criteria were met for three years running:

    1) The name of the meeting remains constant;

    2) The title of the proceedings remains constant; and,

    3) The issues lack a distinctive title.

It was recognized that we would lose access to individual editors, locations, etc., but if a conference had truly stabilized, we felt serials treatment was acceptable. If a conference didn't meet the three criteria or if there was any doubt, it would receive monographic treatment.

The technical services librarians recognized the special circumstances presented by the Institute of Electrical and Electronics Engineers proceedings and agreed that all IEEE conferences would be cataloged as monographs, except when the item is clearly serial in nature. When there is the slightest doubt, we would treat the conference as a monograph.

As you may know, IEEE assigns a unique number to each item, commonly referred to as the "CH" number. These numbers are clearly indicated on all IEEE materials and are frequently cited in the scientific and technical literature. Patrons often approach the reference desk with little more than this number. In the LSM manual environment we maintained a paper file of IEEE publications arranged by CH number, which the public service librarians found invaluable. Having this number as an access point in the online system seemed essential; therefore, it was decided that it would always be entered in a searchable field. We decided to use field 799, a standard MARC field, and believed that adding these fields would not impede the copy cataloging workflow. Based on statistics from previous years, we estimated that 600 items per year would require this special treatment.

The other major recommendation by the task force was to catalog conference proceedings as a set with analytics whenever possible. Now, as I mentioned earlier, we had some internal problems with semantics. Because the term "cat/set/a" was so firmly associated with series treatment, we proposed a new term: "conference call number." The majority of our conference proceedings are received as serials, and our check-in records provide processing instructions. Serials staff would indicate the conference call number on the processing form sent to cataloging with each item. The term "cat/set/a" would no longer be associated with conferences.

The final recommendation of the conference proceedings task force was that when a treatment change is under consideration (e.g., if LC changes to a serials treatment for a conference that had previously received monographic treatment, such as the earlier ACM example), the cataloger should consult with the appropriate science bibliographer. Based on previous years' work, we estimated that about 300 items per year would fall into this category.

And so, our basic recommendations were the following:

- follow LC when the established criteria were met;

- if there is any doubt, treat the conference as a monograph;

- treat all IEEE proceedings as monographs, except when the conference is clearly serial in nature;

- keep conferences together on the shelf with a "conference call number"; and,
- catalogers and science librarians have to talk to each other when changes are being considered.

We recognized that the changes we proposed—increased communication and added access points—might slow the processing of science conference proceedings. We believed that this was an acceptable trade-off for enhancing access to these materials. With the new approach, the science librarians would have input into treatment decisions for the collections they develop, and everyone involved would have the opportunity to learn more about another perspective. Once this kind of communication became routine, we expected that the consultation process would be informal and straightforward.

As I mentioned earlier, there was another task force also at work at Rutgers. This task force was looking at the handling of special issues of journals, which often contain conference proceedings. Sometimes conference proceedings are published in a journal that we subscribe to. Or, sometimes science librarians will purchase a single issue of a journal expressly because it contains conference proceedings. How should we provide access to these individual issues? The situation is complicated because the Rutgers libraries are spread across three main campuses, and we all share an online system. Figure 5 is the IRIS Library System record for the *Journal of Reproduction and Fertility*, which is owned by the Dana Library on the Newark campus and by LSM.

What do we do when a single issue of the journal has conference proceedings to which we want to provide access? The answer to this question might seem relatively obvious: just catalog the special issue as an individual monograph. However, in a large technical services operation, we have to have some governing principles to keep the system humming. We are all struggling with diminished resources, and sadly the days of "curbside" cataloging are over. On the other hand, we don't want to put the cart before the horse: we don't want technical services practices driving collection development decisions. As one science librarian pointed out, "There's no point in buying something that no one will ever be able to find."

Fortunately, we were able to find solutions to the dilemma presented by special issues of journal publications. Because we want to support the collection development decisions of our bibliographers, the guiding principle was defined as: if a science selector makes a deliberate decision to purchase a single issue of a journal and the issue has a distinctive title, it will be cataloged individually, as a separate monograph, and shelved

---

FIGURE 5

Title search for: Journal of Reproduction and Fertility.

102   RUTGERS UNIVERSITY   -IRIS LIBRARY SYSTEM   ALL *TITLE SEARCH

Citation 1 of 26

AUTHOR Society for the Study of Fertility.
TITLE Journal of Reproduction and Fertility.
PUBLISHER [Cambridge, Eng., etc] : Journal of Reproduction and Fertility [etc.]

Library has:
LSM PER   SHELVED BY TITLE   v.1- 1960-
DANA PER   SHELVED BY TITLE   v.9- 1965-

FIGURE 6

Keyword search for: PIG REPRODUCTION NOTTINGHAM

102   RUTGERS UNIVERSITY   -IRIS LIBRARY SYSTEM   ALL *BOOLEAN SEARCH

Citation 1 of 1

AUTHOR   International Conference on Pig Reproduction (3rd : 1989 : University of
            Nottingham School of Agriculture, Sutton, Bonington, UK)

TITLE   Control of pig reproduction III : proceedings of the Third International Conference
          on Pig Reproduction, held at University of Nottingham School of Agriculture,
          Sutton, Bonington, UK, April 1989 / edited by D.J.A. Cole, G.R. Foxcroft and
          Barbara J. Weir.

PUBLISHER Cambridge, U.K. : Journal of Reproduction and Fertility, 1990.

DESCRIP iv, 396 p. : ill. ; 26 cm.

SERIES Journal of reproduction and fertility. Supplement, no. 40.

| | Loan | Call | Cpy | |
Location	Type	Number	#	Status
LSM	STACKS	SF396.9.I57 1989	1	In Library

---

in one of our classified collections rather than in our alphabetically-shelved periodicals collection. For example, Figure 6 is the IRIS Library System record for a special issue of the *Journal of Reproduction and Fertility*.

This record was retrieved using the keywords "pig reproduction Nottingham." A link is provided to the journal with a series tracing.

As I mentioned before, if a selector purchases a special issue, it will be cataloged individually and shelved as if it were a monograph. However, we will not take special issues out of a serial run, nor will we provide analytic monographic cataloging for a single issue *within* a serials run. If access is needed to an individual issue of a journal that Rutgers already subscribes to, a second copy of the issue must be purchased. While it may seems extravagant to purchase second copies in these times of diminished resources, we thought that this solution was very practical. Providing individual access only for items that are purchased as deliberate collection development decisions is, we believe, an elegant solution to a thorny problem.

Summary of Recommendations for Single Issues of Journals:

1) individual cataloging will be provided only for issues with distinctive titles;
2) individual cataloging will be provided for single issues that are purchased as the result of deliberate collection development decisions;
3) single issues will not be plucked from serial runs; and,
4) if it is important enough to catalog, it's important enough to purchase.

Throughout this process of examining practices for conference proceedings and special issues of journals, we explored several complex issues. One question that arose was whether or not science libraries are well served by shared cataloging. In many ways our cataloging practices are driven by the economies of shared cataloging. Few institutions can manage the volume of materials we do without relying on shared cataloging. The Library of Congress provides us with most of our cataloging copy, and we are grateful. However, with all due respect, LC is not a science library in the strictest sense. It supports all the disciplines, and it does so with catalogers who have solid subject backgrounds. But because of this mix in disciplines, it means that some of the values that are important in the sciences cannot be accommodated.

I cannot help but wonder whether science librarians have not ceded control of science literature. Music librarians, for example, frequently point to the special nature of their materials. Cannot similar arguments be made by science librarians? Is there any other discipline that has the complex publishing practices that we find in the sciences? We have series, sub-series, conference proceedings, technical reports, and grey literature, and, in terms of usability, time is of the essence. Science materials present some of the greatest cataloging challenges, and with obvious exceptions such as in geology or the history of science, current materials are valued above all.

Looking at our technical processing practices made us think about the goals of library automation. What is the driving force? Speedier processing? Enhanced access to materials? In some cases we found that the card catalog actually provided more access points. The old paper file of CH numbers for IEEE publications was one example. But another example that I found simply astonishing was that some of our veteran science librarians indicated that occasionally, in the old days, if they determined additional access points were warranted, they would copy a card and type the added entry across the top. I am sure by now you have all read or heard about Nicholson Baker's article in *The New Yorker*. Well, he was wrong about some of the details, but he hit the mark when he talked about librarians who knew both their disciplines and their patrons, librarians who went out of their way to create eminently syndetic and usable card catalogs. We should not expect less of our online systems.

Have we achieved conference proceedings Nirvana at Rutgers? Of course not. Some of the task force's recommendations have yet to be implemented. In part, this is because Rutgers is a large organization, and change takes time. Also, our tight budget situation has meant that certain people who would have had key roles in this transition have taken on other responsibilities. It is a difficult time. However, the main thing is that the science librarians feel that they have been heard and we have established a new standard for problem solving.

As we look to the future, we know that electronic publishing and distribution on the Internet will play a larger role in scholarly communication. And, as we struggle to invent paradigms for providing description and access in this new environment, I believe we can draw on our experiences with providing access to the conference literature. Could I find that conference on fractals in Borneo on the Internet today? I don't think so. I would have to get to the right gopher server and the right directory. In other words, I would have to know where to look. For the Internet to be a serious tool for significant research, someone has to provide both the links and the control over the language, also known as authority control. There is a role here for science librarians, for librarians who have a feel for the discipline and who understand the research practices of their primary clientele.

In closing, let me say that solutions can be simple, and that the most important thing is for public services and technical services librarians to work together. Sometimes it seems that we have all become so specialized that we have lost our common language. However, if we can keep some of the basics of librarianship in mind—public service, access points, standards—we will be able to do what we do best: organize and document the human record in any medium.

Problems with Conference Proceedings: A Public Services Perspective

Loren D. Mendelsohn and James A. Ruffner

Conferences represent an important part of scholarly communication, particularly in science and technology. A brief examination of the directory *Scientific Meetings* will show that, over the course of a year, large numbers of conferences are held covering nearly every subject area in the sciences. In terms of publication of the proceedings of these conferences, one generally can observe a similar pattern. Large numbers of conference proceedings are published in nearly every scientific discipline. Both the number of conferences held and the number of proceedings published tend to reflect the significance of conferences within a particular discipline. There are, however, some notable exceptions. The large number of conferences and proceedings in medical sciences far outweighs their significance to the subject, while the comparatively small number of conferences in computer sciences seems disproportionate to their great significance to that subject. Some rough data supporting these conclusions can be seen in Figures 1 and 2. Additional data are represented in Figure 3. Especially significant are the citation data for computer science disciplines (neural networks and parallel processing), which clearly show the importance of conference literature in this field. With these data in mind, one can more easily understand the pattern of patrons' demand for conference literature.

Patrons request assistance in locating conference literature for two reasons. First, conference literature is inherently difficult to locate. Even when all the information in the patron's citation is accurate, there still can be many significant difficulties. These difficulties can be overcome partially by instructing the patrons in use of appropriate information resources; however, many patrons will still require assistance. Second, because of the source of most citations to the conference literature, patrons will need

FIGURE 1

Conference Subject Distribution

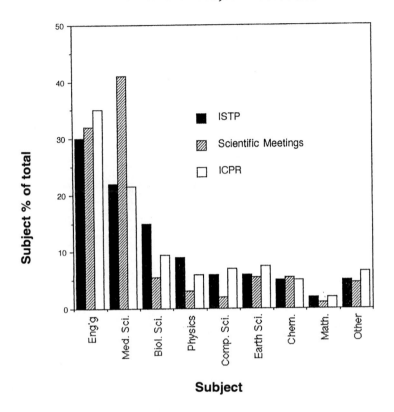

Subject

FIGURE 2

Journal Publication of Conference Papers

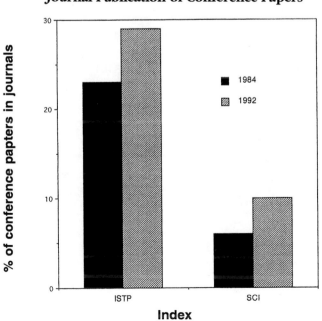

Index

TABLE 1

A Comparison of Type of Source Citations from 10 Conference Papers and 10 Corresponding Journal Papers

Subject	Conference Papers (10 in each subject)					Journal Papers (10 in each subject)				
	Conference	Journal	Books[a]	Other[b]	Total	Conference	Journal	Books[a]	Other[b]	Total
Beta Glucosidase	5	276	23	4	308	2	272	30	2	306
Nuclear Physics	22	175	13	21	231	13	277	11	22	323
Nonlinear Optical Polymers	31	140	25	11	207	32	231	32	9	304
Neural Networks	29	76	37	15	157	57	124	57	15	253
Parallel Processing (IEEE sources)	39	63	15	42	159	73	117	39	34	263
Parallel Processing (ACM Sources)	73	44	23	48	188	118	69	39	34	260
Laser Optics	68	48	2	21	139	26	75	13	12	126
Experimental Mechanics (modal analysis)	49	45	8	17	119	23	68	31	12	141
Hazardous Materials (soil pollution)	24	39	27	36	126	18	105	29	29	181
Battery Technology	32	22	3	16	76	23	39	15	19	96
Totals	372	928	176	231	1,707	385	1,377	295	195	2,252

[a] Excludes known conference proceedings.
[b] Technical reports, dissertations, codes, standards, regulations, personal communications, etc.

assistance in verification. Patrons tend to make somewhat less use of indexing and abstracting services and greater use of journal article or conference paper bibliographies. Thus the majority of requests will be for conference papers that have been cited in various bibliographies. Several studies have indicated that there are significant error rates in such bibliographies (see, for example, Broadus, 1983; Eichorn and Yankauer, 1987; Hernon and Metoyer-Duran, 1992; Satyanarayana and Ratnakar, 1989). Additionally, many citations, while without error, will be incomplete. Thus the primary responsibility of the reference librarian will be verification. Only then can he or she proceed to the task of locating the requested paper.

There are numerous tools that can be helpful for both of these tasks. InterDok's *Directory of Published Proceedings* is published in three series: Science, Engineering, Medicine, and Technology (Series SEMT); Social Sciences and Humanities (Series SSH); and Pollution Control and Ecology (PCE), which is a subset of Series SEMT. These are published monthly with an annual cumulation. Additionally, they are searchable on Data-Star/Dialog (file DOPP). The InterDok Corporation also provides an acquisition service for purchasing the conference proceedings listed in their directory. The *Directory* has three indexes: editor, location, and subject/sponsor. It indexes only down to the level of the conference proceedings, not to the level of individual papers. The entries include location and date of the conference, name of the conference, editor(s), publisher, price, title if different from conference name, and (if available) the ISBN and the Library of Congress control number. Additionally, if the proceedings were published as an issue of a journal, the ISSN, title, volume, issue number, and date of the issue will be supplied. [Editors' note: for a more complete discription of this *Directory*, see the paper by Karen Baschkin in this volume.] Another important source, the *Index to Scientific and Technical Proceedings* published by the Institute for Scientific Information is unique in that it is the only conference literature index that indexes down to the level of individual conference papers. It is published monthly and cumulated annually, and a CD-ROM version is due to be released in late 1994. It indexes meeting location, authors and editors, corporate sponsor and corporate source, and key words in the titles of both the conferences and the individual papers. The indexes refer back to a listing of the tables of contents of the proceedings volumes. While *ISTP* is not comprehensive, ISI makes an effort to identify the most significant published proceedings, using a variety of bibliometric methods. They state in their introduction, "approximately 75% to 90% of the significant conference literature may be expected to appear in *ISTP*." Finally, the *Index to Conference Proceedings* issued by the British Library Document Supply Centre is the closest thing to a comprehensive index for all conference proceedings. It is published monthly with annual cumulations and is also available on CD-ROM. A comprehensive cumulation (1964-1988) is available on microfiche. It is a true index, listing all entries by key word only. As with the *Directory of Published Proceedings,* this is an index of conferences, not of the individual papers presented at the conference. Entries include location and date of the conference, name of the conference, and ISBN if available. When used in conjunction with *Current Serials Received,* also issued by the BLDSC, one can obtain complete information on whether the proceedings were published as a journal issue. Again, the thing to be emphasized about the BLDSC is their effort to be absolutely comprehensive in acquiring their materials. Other useful indexes include the INSPEC set of indexes and databases (*Physics Abstracts, Computing and Control Abstracts,* and *Electrical and Electronics Abstracts*) and *Engineering Index* (including *Compendex Plus,* the electronic version). These indexes will cover the majority of the commonly requested conference literature, because most of the requests will come from researchers and students in engineering and related applied sciences. Also helpful for the occasional non-engineering request are such indexes as *Biological Abstracts RRM* and *Chemical Abstracts*. Any library that experiences a demand for conference literature will need a strong collection of these indexing and abstracting services. This need is independent of whether or not the library has a strong collection of conference literature.

In order to address requests for conference literature, the reference librarian must be aware of all the possible format variations. Many proceedings are published as special issues of periodicals. Proceedings of recurring conferences are frequently published and sold as either monographs or serials, a phenomenon that is usually reflected in their cataloging. Proceedings also may be published as GPO documents (in both hard copy and microfiche), NTIS documents, technical reports, individual papers, and many other variations. More recently, some conferences have been held over the Internet, with the papers and associated discussions archived on an electronic list or an FTP server. Thus there is a significant portion of the conference literature to be found in the grey literature of science and technology. Not all of these variations are indexed well. Often conference proceedings or papers will be republished or simultaneously published in different formats. Most notorious in this regard are the American Society of Mechanical Engineers papers, which are often republished as journal articles or separate proceedings. The Society of Manufacturing Engineers, the American Institute of Aeronautics and Astronautics, and other associations do the same. More often than not, these associations do not, unfortunately, broadcast their intentions in this regard. Thus, there are few concordances that identify the final locations of such republished papers.

While most citations will be derived from bibliographies, many will be derived from indexing and abstracting services. Patrons using such sources often will have difficulty grasping some of the important details in the entry. Patrons often will insist, for example, that the library provide them with a paper which was published in a foreign language, only to be angry that they cannot read the paper once it is given to them. This can happen no matter how carefully the reference librarian points out this problem at the outset. Many citations listed in indexing services will be to items published only as abstracts, i.e., the complete paper may not be available unless the original author is able and willing to supply it. Many indexing services are so comprehensive that they index materials that are held by very few libraries in the world. Some appear to be held by no libraries at all. In such cases, it may be possible to obtain the item by contacting the indexing service, or again by contacting the author(s) of the paper.

Citations derived from bibliographies tend to have a different set of problems. Citations derived from conference paper bibliographies tend to have more problems than citations derived from journal article bibliographies, probably because the process of preparing a conference paper for publication is somewhat looser than the process of preparing a journal article. The relatively high error rate in such citations, as well as their frequent lack of complete bibliographic information, has already been mentioned. Also, many such citations will make extensive use of abbreviations. While some of these abbreviations can be located in standard reference sources, many others will have the appearance of having been invented on the spot in order to complete the bibliography, making the process of identifying the conference in question extremely complex. Some citations may be to papers read at conferences, but not necessarily published in the proceedings volume. Indeed, some citations may be to papers read at conferences for which proceedings were never published. In such cases, it is sometimes possible to locate a journal article by the same author(s) that deals with the same subject matter. Occasionally, such journal articles will explicitly state that portions of the paper were presented previously at a conference. Again, it may be necessary to contact the author(s) of the cited paper to get additional information. If worse comes to worst, it may even be necessary to contact the author of the citing paper to untangle badly garbled citations.

Once the reference librarian has verified the citation, he or she can then proceed to the process of providing access. This can be done in two ways: 1) by owning the item needed, or, 2) by obtaining the item through interlibrary loan or a document delivery service. In both cases, the librarian must be able to locate the needed item. A library with a strong proceedings collection will need to be especially concerned with the quality and depth of the cataloging. As mentioned above, many proceedings are published as both special journal issues and as separate monographs. In the interest of saving money, most libraries will purchase conference proceedings in one format only; in such cases, the cataloging must reflect all possible format variations. This is especially the case when proceedings come through as regular journal issues. In such cases, it can be extremely helpful to perform analytical cataloging on these individual issues. The problem, of course, with such analytical cataloging is that it is extremely labor-intensive and costly. While such analytics often cannot be generated for the local catalog, the reference librarian will frequently find them by using one of the major cataloging databases (OCLC, RLIN, etc.) in conjunction with the indexing services mentioned above. Other cataloging issues are related to the other format variations described above. Many libraries, for example, have large conference collections embedded in their government documents collections. Often the materials in such collections are not individually cataloged, since it is far simpler and more cost-effective to tape load the government documents profile than to catalog individually all the items. The point of all this is that reference librarians often must perform complex and difficult searches before they can accurately determine whether or not the library owns a particular conference proceedings. The more thorough the cataloging, the easier the job of the reference librarian.

The process of locating and verifying holdings for conference literature not owned by the home library can present similar difficulties. Much of this task will have been completed in the process of determining whether or not the item is owned. It can be very helpful during this process to take note of OCLC record numbers, holdings records, cataloging variations, and the like. As mentioned previously, many proceedings of recurring conferences are published, sold, and cataloged as both monographs and serials. These are often among the most frequently requested conferences. IEEE and ACM conference proceedings are good examples of how this can work. Because of the relatively high demand for and the large number of cataloging variations of such proceedings, librarians can find themselves devoting large amounts of time and energy to locating them. The ability of a librarian to locate such proceedings volumes is often dependent on his or her willingness to search through every variant OCLC record. Some libraries will catalog a particular conference series as monographs, generating individual records for every volume, while others will handle the same series as a serial, generating only one record. Occasionally, one can find indications that a particular library's approach to such things changed midstream. Often there will be several serial records, some connected with title changes, and others with local cataloging variations. It is necessary to note all these variations on the document request in order to ensure that the interlibrary loan office has several options for obtaining the requested paper.

The publication of conference proceedings in two formats (journal special issues and monographs) has significant collection development implications. What follows are some rough data showing how the distribution of conference proceedings between these two formats has changed over the years. In 1984, 23% of the conference papers indexed by *ISTP* were published in journals. By 1992, the proportion of *ISTP*-indexed conference papers in journals had increased to 29%. Combining statistics for *ISTP* and *Science Citation Index* leads to an estimate of the percentage of *SCI* journal content devoted to conference papers. In 1984, about 6% of all full length research papers and shorter research notes in *SCI* journals were conference papers. By 1992, nearly 10% of all papers and notes in *SCI* journals were from conference proceedings. These data are summarized in Figure 2. Thus, libraries with major journal collections have a large and increasing number of proceedings, whether specially ordered or not. Since many of these proceedings are published both as special issues or volumes under the journal title and as separate volumes under the conference title, it is important that this double publication be noted bibliographically in OCLC and similar utilities and indexes. Turning the issue around, this analysis of ISI's indexing of both journals and conferences indicates that about 20% of ISI's significant research paper and research note literature is found in "books" and not merely in journals—a striking testimony to the importance of separate conference proceedings. There is more indexing evidence of that importance. Turning to current issues of *Computing and Control Abstracts* and *Engineering Index*, about 33% of the content of each is found in conference proceedings. In the current year's *Index to Conference Proceedings* received by the British Library Document Supply Centre, of 12,000 science and technology conference proceedings, about 3,000 were published in journals and about 9,000 in books.

These data raise some important collection development questions. In order to provide sufficient background for understanding these questions, it is necessary to discuss the seemingly tangential issues of maintenance and deterioration of research collections. The inexorable deterioration of research collections is illuminated in a recent report indicating that ARL libraries collectively provided 5% fewer serial resources and 23% fewer monographs in 1993 than in 1986 (Duval, 1994). This situation has come about for a number of reasons. Faculty members insist that journal subscriptions be maintained at all costs. Also, various forces have pushed for the acquisition of an increasing array of electronic services (often duplicating print sources) and associated hardware. Meanwhile, course reading lists are loaded with basic books that the library is expected to have available. Simultaneously, students (especially foreign students) rely on the library for all sorts of basic materials they simply cannot afford, whether on reading lists or not. This problem is particularly acute in urban universities whose mission is to provide an education to the economically disadvantaged. The consequence is a slow deterioration of journal collections accompanied by very large declines in the acquisition of conference proceedings, expensive research monographs, and treatises that are collected with increasing selectivity to meet current demand only. At the same time, the proceedings content of the journal collection inches forward year by year, so that today approximately $10,000 out of every $100,000 in journal costs represents special issues and volume sets of conference proceedings. That amount (or its appropriate proportion) may be higher than the total available for "one at a time" purchases of research material, yet many of these journal-borne conference proceedings would not pass the cut among proceedings that must be ordered selectively. All these factors lead to a decline in the research strength of library collections.

This preconference is not the place for a rehash of the "serials crisis and decline of research collections" issue. Students must be served with practical texts, handbooks, and methods and techniques literature. The total cost is but a small fraction of the research level effort. Journals are not necessarily the sacred cows of that effort. Biologists, for example, speak very strongly of the primacy of journals, but both they and their students make extremely heavy use of books on methodology and laboratory protocols. Their conference sources can be cut to the bone, so long as we remember to continue purchasing the Cold Spring Harbor Symposia and other sources that our experience tells us are in constant demand. For engineers and others in highly applied fields, conferences represent a very high proportion of the significant primary literature and must be acquired in step with the corresponding journals. The trick is to realize that the total output of journals and conferences in particular fields is (with the exceptions noted above) roughly proportional to their significance. When reductions are made, journals should be cut back as sharply as other research materials. For example, journals whose content is more than 50% conference papers must be examined with special care to see whether the purchase of those proceedings is warranted over against those which must be purchased out of other funds.

It is clear, therefore, that there are profound public service issues created by these changes in publication patterns. How catalogers, indexers, and collection development officers respond to these changes has a significant impact on the ability of the reference librarian to provide access to conference literature. Moreover, because of the budget issues and related pressures described above, how we handle the conference literature can have a profound impact on our ability to provide access to other equally important information sources.

References

Broadus, R. N. (1983). An investigation of the validity of bibliographic citations. *Journal of the American Society for Information Science, 34,* 132-135.

Duval, N. (1994). Current issues: rising prices continue to plague ARL libraries. *ARL: A Bimonthly Newsletter of Research Library Issues and Actions, No. 174,* 1-2.

Eichorn, P., & Yankauer, A. (1987). Do authors check their references? a survey of accuracy of references in three public health journals. *American Journal of Public Health, 77,* 1011-1012.

Hernon, P., & Metoyer-Duran, C. (1992). Literature reviews and inaccurate referencing: an exploratory study of academic librarians. *College and Research Libraries, 53,* 499-512.

Satyanarayana, K., & Ratnakar, K. V. (1989). Accuracy and completeness of references cited in selected biomedical journals. *European Science Editing, No. 36, 5-6. 36,* 5-6.

Why Collect Conference Proceedings?

H. Robert Malinowsky

This paper discusses conference proceedings from the perspective of a collections development officer. Having been a pre-AACR 2 cataloger, I understand well the increasing difficulties that conference proceedings present for catalogers. Automation has helped remarkably in providing access to conference proceedings, but publishers have unsuspectingly created problems by their efforts to market proceedings through as many avenues as possible. These problems have greatly increased the time catalogers have to spend in cataloging proceedings in order to make sure all access points are covered.

Why collect this growing mass of literature? If it is that difficult to identify and catalog, why not just leave the problems to someone else and use interlibrary loan, or wait a year or two until someone else has done all the work of cataloging and then buy the proceedings? That would make it a lot easier for a particular library's catalogers, who may be overworked with other types of cataloging problems. This may sound good, but if everyone did this, no one would have the item, and the researcher would be left holding the bag. Even if the problems of acquiring and cataloging are avoided, there is still the problem of properly identifying the item so that when it is requested by interlibrary loan it is the right proceedings. A researcher may really become upset if, after waiting four weeks or more for an item, the wrong item is received. Therefore, having the proceedings sooner rather than later is one reason to collect proceedings. The purpose of any research collection is to have materials readily available for use with as many access points as possible that are easy to navigate. The University of Illinois at Chicago Library does not collect all available proceedings in the subject areas in which its faculty conducts research. There are just too many of them, and some are too expensive to justify their purchase. However, proceedings are acquired from some major societies and from various other university departments. Some of these proceedings generate major groans in cataloging pre-processing units, especially when a truck of the "blue proceedings" from the Institute of Electrical and Electronics Engineers arrives for processing.

Before the problems of conference proceedings are discussed from a collections development perspective, I will describe briefly how the University of Illinois at Chicago acquires these proceedings.

Several approval plans that include conference proceedings are used. Approximately 40% of the slip selections for the sciences and engineering are for proceedings of conferences. These proceedings may be one-time publications, part of an annual series, or part of a publisher's series. Examples of proceedings offered by Yankee Book Peddler with their approval slips include:

Soil Resilience and Sustainable Land Use, Proceedings (1992, Budapest).
Advances in Underwater Technology, Ocean Science and Offshore.
European Design and Test Conference, 1994.
Institute of Physics Conference Series, no. 138.
AIP Conference Proceedings, 296.

These citations actually were not that difficult for the pre-processing searchers since most had an ISBN. Also, there was other information on the slips that helped to identify each item; however, this list indicates the many ways proceedings can be cited. Here are two more examples that show additional information included on the slips; this information, in turn, generates additional access points:

European Materials Research Society Symposia Proceedings, v. 32 is titled *Materials Surface Processing*, is referred to as the "1992 Strasbourg proceedings," and is a reprint from *Applied Surface Science*, v. 69. In this case, the reprint note is critical to prevent a selector from ordering another copy.

Cellular Automata, Dynamical Systems and Neural Networks, publication date 1994, is referred to as the "1992 Santiago Proceedings," but there is no indication of the name or number of the conference, which turns out to be the Third School on Statistical Physics and Cooperative Systems, held in Santiago, Chile, December 14-18, 1992. Also, note the difference between conference date and publication date.

If the proceedings are part of an identifiable series and it appears that the majority of the items in the series fit the research needs of the institution, a standing order is placed for the series. This is a simple solution, since the individual items do not need verification before ordering. For pre-processing staff, working from an item in hand is much easier than working from a slip or publisher's flyer, although working from a conference proceedings is still more time consuming than working from a simple monograph. Standing orders need to be reviewed on a regular basis because publishers may change their focus without any warning.

Similar to standing orders are blanket orders. Here, a publisher, society, or institute is requested to send everything it publishes. Excellent examples are the blanket orders that the University of Illinois at Chicago has with the Institute of Electrical and Electronics Engineers, American Institute of Physics, and the National Academy of Sciences for their proceedings. IEEE, for example, predicts what it will publish each year, and the library makes a pre-payment at the beginning of the year based on this annual prediction. IEEE then sends its publications, the "blue volumes," at a reduced price, and the library hopes that IEEE holds to its predicted publication schedule. As with standing orders, pre-processing is easier because it is performed with the item in hand.

For individual orders, either a jobber is used or the item is ordered direct. Some jobbers are good at locating proceedings; however, others have disastrous track records. If it is a really difficult item published by an institution or privately published, going direct to the publisher usually assures that the item asked for is the item that will be received. It should be noted that many private institutions require pre-payment.

Finally, there are proceedings received as gifts. Gifts of proceedings are always welcomed because many are obtained as part of an individual's attendance at a conference. Proceedings of this type are not usually for sale to the general public or to libraries. If conference attendees are thoughtful and conscientious, they will keep their institution's library in mind. This type of proceedings is the most difficult to track down when it is encountered in a citation because it was never for sale and CIP copy was never produced. Making sure these proceedings are cataloged expeditiously is important so researchers can benefit.

Now let us look at some specific problems. First, there are a couple of problems that have nothing to do with cataloging. Uppermost in this category is cost. I have already mentioned that proceedings that are out-of-line in cost are usually not purchased. There are proceedings being offered in the sciences that are $600-800 per title for one or two volumes. Some are even more expensive. A library's budget would be placed in jeopardy quickly if very many of these proceedings were purchased. However, if any of these expensive proceedings are purchased, it is beneficial to the research community if they could be cataloged promptly so that they will appear in the local holdings catalog as well as in the national databases—thereby being used locally and nationally.

Timeliness is another important aspect of conference proceedings. Since proceedings are reporting on cutting-edge research, having them published as quickly as possible is important. Proceedings published in 1994 of a meeting held in 1991 will probably not be ordered unless there is a specific request for the item. If these proceedings are acquired, it would be for historical or archival purposes. The researchers who gave the papers will have been in touch with other researchers in their field and will have already shared the papers. However, a word of caution: if no one acquired such proceedings, there would be no copy available for interlibrary loan. One or more of the papers presented at the meeting is bound to be cited and then requested.

Now for some other problems that are of concern and create problems for pre-processing and cataloging units.

Multiple sponsorship sometimes results in proceedings being jointly published by more than one body. Normally this should be no problem. However, let us look at an example: the proceedings of the 7th Workshop on Parallel and Distributed Simulation. This workshop was sponsored by the Association of [i.e., for] Computing Machinery—SIGSIM, the Society for Computer Simulation International, and the IEEE Computer Society. These sponsors all appear neatly on the title page, which is fine if you have the document in hand. What happens if a flyer is received from the Society for Computer Simulation International advertising these proceedings but not indicating that there are two other sponsors? The item does not yet appear on OCLC. The library orders it. When it arrives, a cataloger discovers first that a copy arrived through the blanket IEEE program and, second, by looking at the item, that it is issue number 1 of volume 23 of the "SIGSIM Newsletter" [i.e., *Simulation Digest*], to which the library subscribes. Oh yes, the item ordered is non-returnable. Now the library owns three copies of these proceedings, two of which cost extra while the third was received as part of a serial subscription. It is doubtful that three individuals will want these proceedings at the same time. Why did this happen? One of the sponsors did not properly identify the proceedings as being part of some other publication or indicate that there was more than one sponsor.

Varying names for a series of annual meetings are a problem, as are *variant names* for a single meeting. Retrospective variant and varying names are usually included in authority records and may also be in a bibliographic entry, but a new variant name may or may not be identified before the proceedings of a conference are ordered. A new variant name may make an item look like the proceedings of a brand new conference requiring much additional verification and ultimately a call to the publisher. A good example of a variant name is where two societies co-publish a proceedings but each wants first credit. What do they do? They may simply say IEEE Workshop on Computing if IEEE is marketing the proceedings and ACM Workshop on Computing if the Association for Computing Machinery is marketing them. It is easy to see that these could be two different conferences when they are actually the same conference. Experience has shown that all IEEE and ACM publications need to be verified more than once.

Multiple citations to the same proceedings are another common problem. Simultaneous publication of proceedings as issues of different journals can lead to proceedings being cited in very different ways. This can be problematic for everyone from collections development to cataloging to interlibrary loan. The best way to explain this is to give some examples:

Symposium on Artificial Intelligence and Programming Languages (1977 : University of Rochester). *Proceedings . . .*

Published by ACM separately and as a special issue in each of two serials: *SIGPLAN Notices*, v. 12, no. 8 (August 1977) and *SIGART Newsletter*, no. 64, (August 1977). This one is really not too bad. The serials do exist, and there is only one publisher.

International Conference on Architectural Support for Programming Languages and Operating Systems (3rd : 1989 : Boston, Mass.). *ASPLOS-III Proceedings.*

The proceedings are published jointly by ACM and IEEE. The volume has its own ISBN but it is also an issue of *Computer Architecture News* (v. 17, no. 2, April 1989); of *Operating Systems Review* (v. 23, special issue, April 1989); and of *SIGPLAN Notices* (v. 24, special issue, May 1989). This example is somewhat more complicated, especially if one does not analyze special issues of serials. The proceedings of this conference could have four separate call numbers, thus complicating the instructions for the user who wants to see the proceedings.

Symposium on Architectural Support for Programming Languages and Operating Systems (1982 : Palo Alto, Calif.). *Proceedings.*

This Symposium is also known by the acronym ASPLOS, although "ASPLOS" does not appear in the bibliographic record. This symposium is the first in a series of meetings of which the previous example is the third. These proceedings were published by ACM and appeared in *Computer Architecture News* (v. 10, no. 2, March 1982) and in *SIGPLAN Notices* (v. 17, no. 4, April 1982). Note that these are not designated "special issues."

And finally, consider:

Workshop on Data Abstraction, Databases, and Conceptual Modelling (1980 : Pingree Park, Colo.). *Proceedings . . .*
This Workshop was sponsored by the National Bureau of Standards and others, and appeared in *SIGART Newsletter* (no. 74, January 1981); *SIGMOD Record* (v. 11, no. 2, February 1981); and *SIGPLAN Notices* (v. 16, no. 1, January 1981). In addition, the title page says this is a "special issue," even though each serial title has its own issue number. It is also possible that this could be issued as a government document because of the NBS sponsorship.

All of these examples illustrate potential problems if the item is not cataloged with all possible access points or marketed with the fullest identification possible. The potential for duplication is ever-present. In the above examples, the University of Illinois at Chicago Library has copies of each of the proceedings in each of the publications that were mentioned. The serials cataloger is hard pressed to keep up with all of the conference proceedings published as issues of serials because an attempt is made to analyze all of them as they are received. Unfortunately, if the conference name or the title of the proceedings does not appear on the cover of the serial issue, it may be missed. For those libraries that do not have the proper cataloging expertise, trying to create cataloging records could be very time consuming. Collections development officers are lucky that there are, however, expert catalogers who can provide the detailed cataloging for others to use. Keep in mind that this cataloging expertise is of no use to anyone outside the local institution until the cataloged item appears in OCLC or other databases.

Problems also occur if the spine, cover, and title page titles all are different and are not included in the bibliographic record. Publishers could use any one of these titles in marketing their product; if the title used by the publisher is the one left out in cataloging, then duplication may occur. A sales flyer was recently received from IEEE for some back volumes of proceedings. An advertised title in the flyer was **1989 IEEE Antennas and Propagation Society International Symposium.**

After searching the online catalog, it was discovered that the publication was owned, but that the title was **1989 International Symposium Digest: Antennas and Propagation, San Jose, CA, June 26-30, 1989**, and that the established name of the conference (the name that appeared on the title page of the publication) was: **AP-S International Symposium.** This flyer offered more than fifty items. A considerable amount of time was taken in order to identify each item so that duplicate copies were not ordered. The time would not have been spent if it was not that the titles were being offered at off the original price.

These are some brief thoughts on conference proceedings. It is hoped that they have raised some awareness and that some day there will be standards developed that publishers will follow so that bibliographical control of this literature will be a little easier than it is now. A great deal of my admiration goes out to all of the catalogers who can properly describe this complicated literature. Without these catalogers, collections development officers would be lost, interlibrary loan would be lost, and the researcher certainly would be lost.

Conference Name?
Problems In Identifying
and Obtaining Conference
Publications

Karen Baschkin

I would like to begin with a brief description of the publications and services of InterDok Corporation. For those of you who are not familiar with InterDok, it is the publisher of the *Directory of Published Proceedings*, which is in its thirtieth year of publication. The *Directory* is available in several different series: *Series SEMT: Science/Engineering/Medicine/Technology, Series SSH: Social Sciences/Humanities, Series PCE: Pollution Control/Ecology,* and *Series M/LS: Medical/Life Sciences*. Simply put, it is a bibliographic index to past conferences, meetings, and symposia, and any published material that is a result of a conference. Subscribers use the *Directory* to verify conference information and to locate the literature in order to purchase it for their holdings. The *Directory* includes all information needed to verify, locate, and order the published literature. It does not include any conference citation unless all of the information has been verified by InterDok editorial staff. In addition to being published in a journal format, the *Directory* is available online through Data-Star.

InterDok also publishes *MInd: The Meetings Index*, a future meetings directory. Now in its eleventh year, *MInd* cites future national and international meetings in the fields of science, engineering, medicine, and technology. InterDok also has an acquisitions department, whose staff research and, as a vendor, supply customers with published conference literature, even those hard-to-find materials. In addition, InterDok offers its customers a specialized standing order service, which provides them with ongoing conference materials by conference name, by society, or even by subject.

While InterDok is not involved with the cataloging of conference material, its staff does eat, breathe, and live conferences. Researching and locating conference material can be frustrating, exasperating, and exhausting. If it weren't, this preconference would not be taking place and InterDok would not be as successful as it is!

It is now much easier to research and locate conference material because of the extensive cataloging and indexing efforts of numerous libraries, information centers, and specialized publishers. However, even with these developments, it continues to be difficult to properly identify conference literature. I will share some of the problems that confront InterDok staff, both in identifying the conference material for the *Directory* and in supplying the actual material to InterDok customers.

One continual and consistent problem is that the name of the actual conference and the title of the published literature often are not the same. This can derail verification if the researcher has only the original conference name or only the published title of the proceedings. In addition, when contacting commercial publishers, there is often a lack of consistency regarding the conference description. Publishers will often use "proceedings of . . ." or "International Conference on . . ." as their catalog entries rather than the substantive part of the conference names (e.g., computer-aided engineering, intl. conf.). Recently I had a problem with a commercial publisher, which has offices in the United Kingdom and the United States. Naturally I had placed our order with the United States office, and that office insisted that the publication was not theirs. I then sent them a copy of their catalog, highlighting the particular item I was trying to purchase. I received a phone call from the publisher, explaining to me that the reason they had not located this item in their database is because the United States office had listed it by the substantive part of the conference name, and the catalog (which had originated from the United Kingdom office) had the item listed as "4th proceedings of . . .". She then explained that the two offices of this publisher maintain separate databases of their publications, each having completely independent ways of listing the same titles. I eventually did receive the book, but not without several weeks of exasperating and migraine-inducing telephone calls.

Another problem that arises is the lack of coordination between main sponsoring organizations and their regional groups, which are often the actual distributors. InterDok staff ran into a problem several years ago when they were attempting to trace the proceedings of a conference that had been sponsored by a Florida chapter of the American Society of Mechanical Engineers. We had no luck in our initial attempts to locate the contact name and address for the ASME Florida section and finally called the ASME main office, assuming that they would have the address. Not only did they not have the address of the Florida section, they insisted that there was no Florida section! Finally we located the address of the Florida section's chair, and, as you can imagine, he was somewhat dismayed to hear that the ASME main office had denied knowing of the section's existence. To add insult to injury, the ASME acronym appeared right on the front cover of the publication, in fairly large print.

The inconsistent sponsoring and/or publishing of a repetitive conference is another problem faced when researching conference material. Many times the sponsor of an international conference changes from year to year. This can cause problems in trying to locate any information regarding a particular meeting. There can also be difficulty when a conference and its subsequent publication not only are sponsored by two or more societies, but also the proceedings are published and distributed by several societies. One of the most obvious problems can be seen with the pricing of the proceedings. More often than not, each society charges a different price for the publication. With today's economy and budget problems, libraries obviously want the best price they can obtain without having to contact several societies.

An extremely troublesome problem concerns the publishing of the same proceedings as part of a journal and as a monograph. A library may already have the conference publication in its holdings and not be aware of this when a request is made for the conference. Was the conference material published as part of a book series? Again, the library may already have the material in its holdings. Then there are those proceedings that are published as monographs and also as issues of journals. InterDok has an unwritten rule in its acquisitions department: if conference material ordered by a customer is found to be included in a journal or as part of a series, the department will not supply it until it has confirmation to supply from the customer. We do not want to duplicate a library's holdings. Then there is always the situation when the literature has been published in a variety of ways. There may have been a set of preprints or abstracts that was available at the conference or in advance of the conference and only attainable from the conference organizer. Moreover, the full proceedings may eventually be published by another source.

The time-lag between the year that the conference was held and the year that the proceedings are actually published is also problematic. Some proceedings volumes are available before the meeting, some are available at the meeting, and the rest (we hope) become available after the meeting. Usually meetings that are sponsored and whose proceedings are published by the same organization are available within a reasonable amount of time. Very often proceedings that are sponsored by one society or organization and then published by another may take several years before they are available. Furthermore, when proceedings have been published as a multiple-volume set, there are numerous times when the first two volumes are available and the third volume does not become available for quite some time. Probably the most frustrating situation is when there are several different books from the different symposia at the conference, and each is published by a different source. This is your basic research nightmare.

Now that I have highlighted some of the hindrances in researching and locating conference material, how do we solve these problems and actually find the material? Because InterDok deals exclusively with conference material, we have developed an extensive in-house library where we maintain a variety of sources that we utilize in our researching. These sources cover all aspects of research in conference literature (e.g., directories of regional, national, and international organizations; publisher directories; research center directories; corporate directories; future conference directories; and directories of conference collections).

The first step InterDok staff takes when trying to locate a conference publication is to search either InterDok's in-house database or back volumes of the *Directory of Published Proceedings*. The *Directory* includes over 4,000 conference listings per year just in its *Series SEMT: Science/Engineering/Medicine/Technology*. Therefore, after thirty years of publishing, there is a good chance that the conference publication can be located. When researching, the staff also utilizes back issues of *MInd: The Meetings Index,* which are used to verify the conference name, date, and location as well as the sponsor of the conference.

The British Library Document Supply Centre *Index of Conference Proceedings* (formerly *Index of Conference Proceedings Received*) is probably the best collection source for researching conference literature. It is the index to the conference holdings of the BLDSC. InterDok staff have found this to be the most comprehensive of all collections of conference material. Although the *Index* does not include the names and addresses of publishers or distributors, it will verify that the conference material does exist and how it has been published (e.g., abstracts, preprints etc.), as well as steer the researcher in the right direction towards locating the published material.

When trying to locate conference literature, researchers should always use future meetings directories to aid in their research as InterDok staff does with *MInd: The Meetings Index*, *World Meetings*, and *International Congress Calendar*. All of these are excellent sources and can be used to locate the sponsoring organization when all the researcher has is the name and date of the conference. Once contacted, the sponsor can usually lead the researcher to the correct publisher or distributor of the proceedings.

In addition to the various online databases (e.g., OCLC), there are other sources that can be used, including *Proceedings In Print*, which is another bibliography of past conferences and the subsequent literature; *Conference Papers Index* issued by Cambridge Scientific Abstracts; and *Index to Scientific & Technical Proceedings*. Both the Cambridge Scientific Abstracts publication and *ISTP* are excellent sources for locating individual papers. The one drawback to *ISTP* is that it includes only those conference publications that "contain complete papers, not just abstracts". The concern with this limitation is that many times all that has been published is the book of abstracts, and many libraries will want whatever is available. By limiting the inclusions of conference material, one tends to increase the exclusions. In a field so erratic as the researching of conference literature, often it is preferable to include rather than exclude.

Now that you have a general idea of some of the sources a researcher can use to verify and/or locate published conference material successfully, I believe it would be useful for me to provide the following list of steps any researcher should use to verify and locate a conference publication.

1)   Verify the conference name, date, and location. Once you have verified the name, date and location of the conference, you should be able to continue your research in the right direction.

2)   Locate the sponsor of the conference. The sponsor should then be able to lead you right to the distributor.

3)   At this point, if you find yourself at a dead end, there are several options:

a)   Call InterDok. InterDok staff love a good challenge!

b)   Try to locate the previous conference in its conference series. There may be information in the foreword or preface that could help you in your research (e.g., a sponsor of the previous conference may have information on a subsequent conference). Also, the editor of the previous conference volume may have information on the subsequent conference. Many times repetitive conference publications are edited by the same editor(s).

c)   If you absolutely can go no further with your searching, try to locate a society or association that is in the same field of interest as the conference. Societies that are very specific in nature tend to have information on conferences that are held in their fields of interest.

In conclusion, I hope that this paper has shed some light on the mysteries of verifying and locating conference literature and how to solve them. The means of researching conference material has improved greatly over the past fifteen years, particularly with the advent of electronic databases. I expect that with more conference collections being made available and their increased accessibility though online databases, the success of locating and obtaining conference proceedings will only continue to improve.

APPENDIX A
Library of Congress Rule Interpretations Relating to Conference Proceedings: A Chronology and Summary

Daniel W. Kinney

The issues of the *Cataloging Service Bulletin* cited should be consulted for complete texts of the Library of Congress Rule Interpretations and examples. References to the texts of the cataloging rules are to page numbers in the 1988 revision of the *Anglo-American Cataloguing Rules*, second edition.

1. Name of Conference (LCRI 21.1B1)

1981   A capitalized phrase is considered a name even if it is preceded by an indefinite article (only the definite article is specified in the text of AACR 2) when it is in a language that capitalizes each word in a name. The phrase must also include a word that denotes a meeting in order to be considered a named conference. This interpretation can apply only to languages that capitalize each word of a name even in running text (CSB 14 (1981): 18).

1982   The definition of a conference in footnote 1 is interpreted to include named meetings entered directly and named meetings entered subordinately to a heading for a corporate body. A meeting of a corporate body is treated as a named meeting if it consists of a generic term or of a generic term plus one or more of the following elements: the venue of the meeting; number, date, or other sequencing element (CSB 15 (1982): 8–9). A meeting of a corporate body is treated as named if it consists of a generic term plus the name of the holding body (cf. LCRI 24.13, type 5 (type 6 in AACR 2 (1988)). A name consisting of one or more of these elements that is either a meeting of two or more corporate bodies or a meeting of a committee, commission, board, or similar body (e.g., a panel, task force, work group) is an exception and is not treated as a named meeting (CSB 18 (1982): 30–31).

1983   Generic-term names of meetings that designate a meeting *of* a body (e.g., Annual Meeting) are considered named meetings when they appear in relation to the name of the body, whether or not the generic term is strengthened by the name or an abbreviation of the name of the body. Generic-term designations for *sponsored* meetings are considered named only if the name, an abbreviation of the name, or some other distinctive noun or adjective strengthens the generic term. Determine the form of the name according to the appropriate provisions of Chapter 24 (e.g., 24.7; 24.13, type 3; 24.13, type 5 (type 6 in AACR 2 (1988)). Rule 24.7 deals with additions to conference headings (see section 5). Rule 24.13 deals with subordinate and related bodies entered subordinately (see section 6) (CSB 22 (1983): 22–23).

2. Conference Name as Main Entry (LCRI 21.1B2)

1981   The three conditions applied in determining whether or not a work emanates from a corporate body (cf. AACR 2 (1988), 313, footnote 2) are explained in LCRI 21.1B2 (CSB 12 (1981): 21–22). Catalogers are to assume that a corporate body is involved with a work if there is doubt that the work emanates from the corporate body (CSB 14 (1981): 19). In order for a work that emanates from a conference to be entered under the heading for that body, the name of the conference must appear prominently on the publication being cataloged. Reference is made to AACR 2 rule 0.8 in which the word "prominently" means that the information is found in a formal statement in the prescribed sources of information for areas 1 and 2. For books, the prescribed sources of information for the title and statement of responsibility area (area 1) and the edition area (area 2) are the title page, other preliminaries, and colophon. The preliminaries are defined as "the title page(s) of an item, the verso of the title page(s), any pages preceding the title page(s), and the cover." (AACR 2 (1988), 621). The predominant content or purpose of the work is considered in judging whether the work falls into one of the categories of 21.1B2 (Category d applies to conference proceedings). If there is some material that does not fall into one of the categories, it may be ignored for the purpose of making the determination. If there is any doubt as to whether a work falls into one or more of the categories, the involvement of the corporate body is ignored in determining the main entry (CSB 12 (1981): 22–24).

1991   The name of the conference must appear on the chief source of information in order for conference proceedings to be entered under the heading for the conference. This LC policy is a change from previous practice in which the name of the conference just had to appear prominently as defined in rule 0.8 (CSB 54 (1991): 34).

3. Conference Name as Added Entry (LCRI 21.1B3, LCRI21.30E)

1981   An added entry is made for a conference named anywhere in the item when the proceedings are not entered under the heading for the conference because the name of the conference does not appear prominently according to LCRI 21.1B2d (CSB 14 (1981): 22).

1991   An added entry is made for a conference named *prominently* in the item when the proceedings are not entered under the heading for the conference because the name of the conference does not appear on the *chief source of information* (see LCRI 21.1B2d) (CSB 54 (1991): 35).

1992   The Library of Congress Rule Interpretation for 21.1B3, which was stated in CSB 14 and 54 (see above), is canceled, and the added entry for a conference is covered by LCRI 21.30E. The text from CSB 54 is reproduced under LCRI 21.30E, and 1991 practice remains in effect (CSB 56 (1992): 13).

1993   An added entry is made for a conference named *anywhere* in the item when the proceedings are not entered under the heading for the conference, because the name does not appear on the chief source of information (CSB 60 (1993): 16).

4. Added Entry for the Sponsor of a Conference (LCRI 21.30E)

1981   An added entry is made for a corporate body that sponsors a conference if the work is entered under the heading for the conference and the body is prominently named, or if the work is entered under title and the sponsoring body is named anywhere in the item (CSB 12 (1981): 25).

1991   An added entry is made for a corporate body that sponsors a conference when the body is prominently named (CSB 54 (1991): 35).

5. Serial vs. Monograph Treatment of Conference Proceedings (LCRI 12.0A)

1983   Conference publications are cataloged as serials only if: 1) the name of the meeting remains constant; and, 2) the title remains constant and in the same language. Both criteria must be met and must be demonstrable for five consecutive issues and within a period of no more than 15 years (CSB 20 (1983): 9–10).

1986   As in the 1983 rule interpretation, the name and title of the meeting must remain constant in order for a conference publication to be treated as a serial, but these two criteria can be documented by evidence in several issues of the item, in bibliographies, or in the catalog against which the item is being cataloged. The number of issues, consecutiveness, and a fixed span of time are no longer specified. All other conference publications (i.e., those that do not meet *both* criteria) are cataloged as monographs, even if there is evidence that the conference is held repeatedly (CSB 32 (1986): 19).

1989   A third criterion is added to the conditions stipulated in 1986. The publication must *not* have a distinctive title. All three conditions must be met in order for a conference publication to be treated as a serial. Once a conference publication has been treated as a serial, earlier and later title changes are also cataloged as serials (CSB 44 (1989): 26–27).

1990   The third condition (i.e., the issues do not have individual titles) is defined as the lack of "specific titles that necessarily vary from conference . . . to . . . conference . . ." (CSB 50 (1990): 30).

6. Additions to Headings for Conferences (LCRI 24.7B)

1982   The number, date, and place are *not* added to headings in authority records for both ongoing conferences entered directly under their own names and ongoing conferences entered subordinately to headings for corporate bodies. If the name of an ongoing conference conflicts, an appropriate qualifier is added to the heading in the authority record. In bibliographic records for conference publications, the local place or institution, etc., that appears with the conference name in the source for the conference name is used as an addition to the heading (24.7B4). If both the institution and the local place name appear in the source, the name of the institution is preferred as the addition to the heading. The local place name is not added unless the name of the institution is a very weak one (CSB 15 (1982): 24–25). The name of an institution is given in the nominative case in the language in which it is found on the item. The name of a local place is given its catalog-entry form as modified by 23.4A and 24.4C1 (second paragraph). The name of a hotel, convention center, or an office building is not used as a location unless the conference was held outside a local place (CSB 18 (1982): 75). An item containing the proceedings, etc., of two meetings of the same conference for which main entry under the conference is appropriate is entered under the heading for the first conference. An added entry is made for the second conference even if the meetings are consecutively numbered (CSB 15 (1982): 25).

1983   When the name of the conference includes the year, the year must be repeated if the name is followed by one or more additions (e.g., Datafair '75 (1975 : London, England). An item containing the proceedings, etc. of three or more meetings of the same conference is entered under the heading for the conference without any additions (CSB 21 (1983): 29–30).

7. Conferences Entered Subordinately to Headings for Corporate Bodies (LCRI 24.13)

1982   LCRI 24.13, type 3: Names that are "empty" (i.e., names that do not contain distinctive elements or subject words) and names that only indicate the location or a numeric or alphabetic designation are entered under the higher body. LCRI 24.13, type 5: A named meeting that contains the entire name of a corporate body is entered subordinately to the heading for the corporate body if the name of the meeting contains the name used in the heading for the corporate body and no more than a generic term for the meeting or no more than a generic term and one or more of the following elements: the venue of the meeting, number, date, or other sequencing element. A named meeting is entered directly under its own name in all other cases (CSB 15 (1982): 25–27).

1984   Rule 24.13, type 3 is replaced with what is essentially the current text of the rule in AACR 2 (1988). LC interprets "a name that is general in nature" to mean a name that contains "neither very distinctive elements (such as proper nouns or adjectives) nor subject words" (e.g., Annual Meeting) (CSB 25 (1984): 67–68).

1989   In AACR 2 (1988), the rule that was formerly 24.13, type 5 becomes 24.13, type 6. The LC rule interpretation for named meetings containing the entire name of a corporate body, which was originally published in 1982 for 24.13, type 5, remains the same and is applied to 24.13, type 6 (CSB 44 (1989): 61-62). An explanation of the reasons behind the Library of Congress Rule Interpretations for the two types of named meetings entered subordinately under a corporate body was published in CSB 28 (1985): 21–23.

APPENDIX B
Recommendations for Publishers of Conference Proceedings

Prepared by the ACRL Science and Technology Section

In 1984 the ACRL Science and Technology Section formed an ad hoc Committee on Designing a Conference Proceedings Style Sheet. Committee members included Dorothy McGarry (chair), Grace Agnew, Carol Cubberley, Edward Garten, and Sara Shatford Layne.

Given the problems found in cataloging and identifying conference proceedings, the committee thought it would be useful to prepare recommendations that will assist editors and publishers in the preparation of proceedings for publication. A draft of these recommendations appeared in the February 1986 issue of *College & Research Libraries News*. Based on feedback from ACRL members, the Committee revised the draft. The STS Executive Committee approved the draft in January 1987 and reaffirmed their approval in January 1989.

Recommendations
Published proceedings of conferences are very important in research. It is often difficult, however, for people to locate the proceedings of a particular meeting. Often the title pages of these proceedings are confusing in their layout, or the title pages contain insufficient information for identifying a particular conference. This is critical because the title page is the established standard source for information used to catalog a book. The librarians who catalog the book and the library users who request it may not be sure what the title is intended to be, or who published the book, or even what the name of the meeting is. This confusion and uncertainty make it difficult for library users to know how to cite the book or how to look for it in a catalog.

Those who prepare and publish conference proceedings should contribute to the usefulness of the conference literature by applying the following guidelines:

Title page

The title page should include:
- A clearly indicated title.
    Examples:
    Microcomputer software
    Modern problems of surface physics.
- Clearly indicated information beyond that of the title itself, including information such as the name of the meeting if it had a name.
    Example:
    Proceedings of the Working Conference on Circulation, Neurobiology, and Behavior, held October 4–7, 1981, in Dallas, Texas, U.S.A.
- The relationship of the book to the conference should be indicated on the title page.
    Examples:
    Proceedings of the 23rd IEEE Conference on Decision & Control
    Selected papers from the Workshop on . . .
- Layout and typography can assist in identifying the various elements of information required.
- Include the number of the meeting if any, and the place and date the meeting was held.
- Name of sponsoring organization(s), with an explicitly statement such as "sponsored by" or "organized by".
- An explicit description of function with the name(s) of the editor(s), such as "edited by", or "chairman/editor".
- Series statement, if the publication is part of a series, with clearly indicated series title and numbering.
- Place(s) of publication, name(s) of publisher(s), and date(s) of publication.

Confusion can arise depending on how information appears on the title page; i.e., the initials of the conference may appear at the top of the page followed by the name of the conference or "Proceedings of the..." followed by words which might actually be the book's title meant by the publisher or the editor. A library may choose a title the publisher or editor didn't intend when describing the book in a catalog, not being sure which of the parts was meant to be the title. The library user may come up with two different citations for the same conference, perpetuating problems in retrieval. As an example: *Proceedings of the Workshop on Geological Disposal of Radioactive Waste* (top of page); *In Situ Experiments in Granite* (middle of page).

This might result in one cataloger putting as the title "Proceedings of the ..." and another using "In situ experiments in granite." In this case, the title on the front cover was "Geological disposal of radioactive waste," which could add to the confusion over what the title was meant to be.

All information on the title page should be consistent with information on the cover and spine; titles should not differ from cover to title page, nor should the name of the meeting nor the title of the series differ from location to location within the book.

Back of the title page

The back of the title page should include: Name and address of distributor, if different from publisher, with an explicit statement of function; e.g., "distributed in the U.S. by," or "available from." and copyright information.

Miscellaneous
Names of conferences
Catalogers attempt to determine, when checking a conference publication, whether the conference is "named" or "unnamed." A book whose title page reads *Semiconductor physics: Proceedings of an International Conference* would not be considered to be the proceedings of a "named" conference while *Proceedings of the International Conference on Semiconductor Physics* would lead to access under the name "International Conference on Semiconductor Physics." In the first case, "an international conference" is taken to be a purely generic description; in the second case, "the International Conference on..." indicates a specifically named event.

In cases where different forms of a conference name appear in different locations, the cataloger must determine whether the name of the conference might be, for example: *Computer Society Conference on Artificial Intelligence Applications* (title page) and *IEEE Computer Society Conference on Artificial Intelligence Applications* (preface).

While in some situations this might not matter much, in putting a record for this work into a catalog for patrons' and librarians' use it is important to remember that the record could appear in any one of three different locations in the catalog. Furthermore, if the conference is one in a series of similar conferences, and each year there is a change in the order of the words in the name, such as *Condensed Matter Physics Symposium: Symposium on Condensed Matter Physics*, the records for these conferences will not appear next to each other in the catalog and the works will not appear next to each other on the shelves.

The name of the conference, if it has one, should appear clearly on the title page, back of the title page, pages before the title page, the cover, or the spine, in order for provision of clear and primary access to that name in bibliographic records; librarians would appreciate it if it actually appeared on the title page. If the name of the meeting does not appear in any of the places mentioned above, access to the name of the conference on a record would depend on whether the cataloger noticed the name elsewhere (e.g., in the preface or introduction) and whether a note and an additional access point were made. Of course, if the meeting has no name as far as the conference arrangers are concerned, it is not necessary to create one.

If a name is used for the conference it should be the same in all locations in the book.

If a name of a conference changes form one meeting to the next, and the intent is that they be considered to be related (e.g., earlier and later name of conferences in a sequence) indicate in the later publication that the name of the previous meeting was different.

Names of corporate bodies
If the name of a corporate body is placed on the title page, provide with it some explanation of the relationship of that body to the conference or to the publication, e.g., "published by," "sponsored by," "organized by," "supported by."

Numbering
If a conference is given a number, and previous conferences in the sequence had no number, provide a list of the conferences, with title, name of conference (if different), and date and where held, so that related conferences can be referred to or linked through cross references.

If conferences are numbered, and the proceedings of a particular conference are not published, provide that information in a later volume.

Number the pages consecutively, if possible.

"Volume" and "edition" have very specific meanings in libraries. "Volume 2," e.g., should not be used for the proceedings of the second conference in a sequence. "Volume" should be used only if the proceedings of a particular conference are published in two or more physical volumes. A statement that call something a "second edition" should refer to the same text reworked or reset, not to totally new text. Proceedings of a second conference would not, therefore, be either a "second edition" or a "volume two" of the first conference.

Although librarians are among the primary collectors of conference proceedings, catalog records, for these proceedings appear in machine-readable database which make the information available to millions of library users. Proper access to these proceedings makes them more valuable to the scientific, academic, and business communities. With the help of those who prepare and publish conference proceedings library users will be able to locate and use those proceedings more efficiently.

Recommendations developed in 1986 by the ACRL Task Force on Conference Proceedings.

APPENDIX C
Bibliographic Control of Conference Proceedings: A Workbook of Exercises/Examples

Prepared by Sara Shatford Layne

With the assistance of Beacher Wiggins, Rebecca S. Uhl, Colby Mariva Riggs, Sarah Mitchell, David W. Mill, Dorothy McGarry, Joan P. Lussky, Daniel W. Kinney, Nirmala S. Bangalore

Example I. "Dentistry"

Exercise:

As a cataloger, use the title page provided here and answer the following questions:

A. What is the main entry for this item and why?

B. What is the name of this conference?

C. What is the title of this item?

D. What information should be included in the title and statement of responsibility (245 field)?

E. What added entries should be made and why?

F. Formulate the qualifier for the conference name.

Notes:

Proceedings

First National Symposium on

Dentistry's Role
and Responsibility
in Mass Disaster
Identification

ADA Headquarters Building
Chicago, Illinois
June 23-24, 1986

Edited by:
Dr. E. Steven Smith
Dr. Raymond D. Rawson

Sponsored by:
The ADA Council on Dental Practice
Northwestern University Dental School
The American Board of Forensic Odontology
The American Society of Forensic Odontology

Title page

American
Dental
Association

211 East Chicago Avenue
Chicago, Illinois 60611

Council on
Dental Practice

Proceedings

First National Symposium on
Dentistry's Role and Responsibility in Mass Disaster Identification

Cover

© 1988 American Dental Association
Printed in U.S.A.

Title page verso

```
    ARN:    3512978
    Rec stat: n        Entered:      19931213
►  Type:      z        Upd status:  a      Enc lvl:   n      Source:    b
    Roman:     ■        Ref status:  a      Mod rec:          Name use:  a
    Govt agn:  ■        Auth status: a      Subj:      a      Subj use:  a
    Series:    n        Auth/ref:    a      Geo subd:  n      Ser use:   b
    Ser num:   n        Name:        n      Subdiv tp:        Rules:     ·c ¶
►   1   010     n 93804520  ¶
►   2   040     DNLM ‡c DLC ¶
►   3   005     19931213070052.1 ¶
►   4   111 20  National Symposium on Dentistry's Role and Responsibility in
Mass Disaster Identification ¶
►   5   411 20  Symposium on Dentistry's Role and Responsibility in Mass
Disaster Identification, National ¶
►   6   670     Its (1st : Chicago, Ill. : 1986). Proceedings, c1988: ‡b t.p.
(First National Symposium on Dentistry's Role and Responsibility in Mass
Disaster Identification, ADA Headquarters Bld. Chicago, IL June 23-24, 1986) ¶
```

Authority record

```
    ARN:    631144
    Rec stat: n        Entered:      19810813
►  Type:      z        Upd status:  a      Enc lvl:   n      Source:
    Roman:     ■        Ref status:  a      Mod rec:          Name use:  a
    Govt agn:  ■        Auth status: a      Subj:      a      Subj use:  a
    Series:    n        Auth/ref:    a      Geo subd:  n      Ser use:   b
    Ser num:   n        Name:        n      Subdiv tp: ■      Rules:     ·c ¶
►   1   010     n 81085913  ¶
►   2   040     DLC ‡c DLC ¶
►   3   005     19840322000000.0 ¶
►   4   110 20  Council on Dental Practice (U.S.) ¶
►   5   410 20  American Dental Association. ‡b Council on Dental Practice ¶
►   6   410 20  ADA Council on Dental Practice ¶
►   7   410 20  A.D.A. Council on Dental Practice ¶
►   8   670     Computers in dental practice, c1981 (a.e.) ‡b t.p. (American
Dental Association/Council on Dental Practice) p. 1 (ADA Council on Dental
Practice) ¶
```

Authority record

```
OCLC:   18307054          Rec stat:     c
Entered:      19880803     Replaced:    19951110      Used:      19930810
▶ Type:  a    ELvl: I    Srce:  d    Audn:        Ctrl:        Lang:  eng
  BLvl:  m    Form:      Conf:  1    Biog:        MRec:        Ctry:  ilu
              Cont:  b   GPub:       Fict:  0     Indx:  0
  Desc:  a    Ills:      Fest:  0    DtSt:  s     Dates: 1988,      ¶
▶   1  040     JAA ≠c JAA ≠d MBU ≠d OCL ¶
▶   2  096     W 705 N277p 1986 ¶
▶   3  090     ≠b ¶
▶   4  049     CLUM ¶
▶   5  111 2   National Symposium on Dentistry's Role and Responsiblity in Mass
Disaster Identification ≠n (1st : ≠d 1986: ≠c Chicago, Ill.) ¶
▶   6  245 10  Proceedings / ≠c First National Symposium on Dentistry's Role
and Responsibility in Mass Disaster Identification, ADA headquarters building,
Chicago, Illinois, June 23-24, 1986 ; edited by E. Steven Smith, Raymond D.
Rawson ; sponsored by the ADA Council on Dental Practice ... [at al.]. ¶
▶   7  260     Chicago, Ill. : ≠b American Dental Association, Council on
Dental Practice, ≠c c1988. ¶
▶   8  300     100 p. ; ≠c 28 cm. ¶
▶   9  504     Bibliography: p. 96-97. ¶
▶  10  650 2   Forensic Dentistry ≠x congresses. ¶
▶  11  700 1   Smith, E. Steven. ¶
▶  12  700 1   Rawson, Raymond D. ¶
▶  13  710 2   Council on Dental Practice (U.S.) ¶
▶  14  740 01  Dentistry's role and responsibility in mass disaster
indentification. ¶
```

Bibliographic record (record altered; may not match OCLC version)

Example II. "Solidification processing"

Exercise:

A. Given the following citation from *Index to Scientific & Technical Proceedings* (ISTP) 1989, how might you search for this conference in catalogs with which you are familiar? That is, what access point(s) would you expect to find in the catalog record for the proceedings of this conference?

> 3rd International Conf on Solidification Processing, Sheffield, England, Sep 21-23, 1987.

B. Compare your access point(s) with those found in the catalog record. Would you have found this record using your access point(s)?

C. Compare the citation in ISTP with the citations from the British Library Document Supply Centre (BLDSC) *Index of Conference Proceedings,* and Metadex. Which ones most closely match the catalog record and the item's title page?

Notes:

Solidification Processing 1987

Proceedings of the
Third International Conference,
organised by the Department of Metallurgy,
University of Sheffield, and held at
Ranmoor House, Sheffield, on
21–24 September 1987

THE INSTITUTE OF METALS
LONDON
1988

Title page

```
    OCLC:   18049724           Rec stat:    p
    Entered:     19880518      Replaced:    19950421      Used:     19950410
 ▶ Type:   a     ELvl:         Srce:        Audn:         Ctrl:         Lang:   eng
    BLvl:  m      Form:         Conf:   1    Biog:         MRec:         Ctry:   enk
                  Cont:  b      GPub:        Fict:   0     Indx:   1
    Desc:  a      Ills:  a      Fest:   0    DtSt:   s     Dates:  1988,     ¶
 ▶  1   010       88-9380 ¶
 ▶  2   040       DLC ǂc DLC ¶
 ▶  3   020       0901462365 : ǂc $90.00 (U.S.) ¶
 ▶  4   050 0     TN690 ǂb .S6113 1988 ¶
 ▶  5   082 0     671 ǂ2 19 ¶
 ▶  6   090       ǂb  ¶
 ▶  7   049       CLUM ¶
 ▶  8   245 00    Solidification processing 1987 : ǂb proceedings of the third
 international conference / ǂc organised by the Department of Metallurgy,
 University of Sheffield, and held at Ranmoor House, Sheffield, on 21-24
 September 1987. ¶
 ▶  9   260       London : ǂb Institute of Metals ; ǂa Brookfield, VT, USA : ǂb
 Institute of Metals, N. American Publications Center, ǂc 1988. ¶
 ▶ 10   300       xi, 552 p. : ǂb ill. ; ǂc 28 cm. ¶
 ▶ 11   500       "Compiled and produced for the University of Sheffield by the
 Institute of Metals"--T.p. verso. ¶
 ▶ 12   504       Includes bibliographies and index. ¶
 ▶ 13   650 0     Solidification ǂx Congresses. ¶
 ▶ 14   710 2     University of Sheffield. ǂb Dept. of Metallurgy. ¶
 ▶ 15   710 2     Institute of Metals. ¶
```

Bibliographic record

1612737   MA Number: 89-620229
Fibre Reinforcement of Aluminium by Squeeze Casting: Summary of the State of the Art.
Jolly, M R ; Haour, G
Battelle Europe
Conference: Solidification Processing 1987, Sheffield, UK, 21-24 Sept. 1987
Publ: The Institute of Metal, 1 Carlton House Terrace, London SW1Y 5DB, UK, 1988
463-467
Journal Announcement: 8904
Language: ENGLISH

Citation from METADEX

SOLIDIFICATION PROCESSING
1987 Sep   Sheffield
  Solidification processing--3rd International
  conference--Papers--University of Sheffield,
  Department of Metallurgy
  ISBN 0901462365 pbk   **2247.800 421**

Citation from BLDSC *Index of Conference Proceedings*

Example III. "Hadronic physics"

Exercise:

As a cataloger, use the title page and preface of each of these two proceedings to answer the following questions:

A. Is the conference named?

      1988 conference:

      1991 conference:

B. If the conference is named, what is the name?

      1988 conference:

      1991 conference:

C. If the conference is named, what kind of access to that name (main, added, or no entry) should be provided in the catalog record?

      1988 conference:

      1991 conference:

D. Look at the citations from INSPEC to papers published in each of these two volumes and to the citations to the proceedings from the BLDSC *Index of Conference Proceedings*. Does the determination you made match the way the proceedings are cited in these two sources? If not, what are the differences?

Notes:

1988 conference

Title page

HADRONIC PHYSICS

Winter School held at Folgaria, Italy
Third Course, February 15-20, 1988

Edited by:

Roberto CHERUBINI

I.N.F.N. - Laboratori Nazionali di Legnaro
Legnaro, Padova
Italy

Pietro DALPIAZ

Dipartimento di Fisica
Universita' di Ferrara
I.N.F.N. - Laboratori Nazionali di Legnaro
Legnaro, Padova
Italy

Bruno MINETTI

Dipartimento di Fisica
Politecnico di Torino
I.N.F.N. - Sezione di Torino
Torino
Italy

1989

NORTH-HOLLAND
AMSTERDAM • OXFORD • NEW YORK • TOKYO

PREFACE

The Third Winter School on "Hadronic Physics" was held on Folgaria (Trento), Italy, on Febraury 15-20, 1988.

The Course, organized by the Laboratori Nazionali di Legnaro - INFN with the generous support of the Istituto Nazionale di Fisica Nucleare (I.N.F.N.), was attended by 86 participants from many institutions, belonging to different disciplines.

The Course with the same aim as of the previous two Schools was focussed on several subjects, including theoretical and experimental nuclear and elementary particle physics, and on related topics concerning detectors, data analysis, particle accelerators and technology underlining the interdisciplinary aspects.

One full day was devoted to underground physics, cosmology and related subjects. Particular emphasis was placed on the experiments planned at the Laboratori Nazionali del Gran Sasso (LNGS), Italy.

The spirit of the School was to guide the freshly graduated physicists how to carry out research and to propose present open problems.

So, the lectures were given at a tutorial level, also for very advanced subjects, as it is reflected in this book.

Thanks are due to the Folgaria Tourist Agency and in particular to Drs. G. Dorigati and Dr. M. Struffi for their assistance in the organization.

Sincere acknowledgements are due to Mrs. C. Zecchin for precious support she gave in organizing the School; to Mr. P. Schiavon for his valuable technical assistance; to Mrs. M. Stefani for her patience and efficient work in respect of manuscript preparation and typing.

R. CHERUBINI
P. DALPIAZ
B. MINETTI

Preface

1991 conference

Title page

Proceedings of the 6th Winter School on Hadronic Physics

Common Problems and Ideas of Modern Physics

Folgaria (Trento), Italy   4 – 9 February 1991

Editors
T. Bressani
B. Minetti
A. Zenoni

 **World Scientific**
Singapore • New Jersey • London • Hong Kong

v

PREFACE

The 6th Winter School on "Hadronic Physics" was held in Folgaria (Trento), Italy from February 4 to February 9, 1991. The Course, organized by the Sezione di Torino of the Istituto Nazionale di Fisica Nucleare (I.N.F.N.), was attended by 85 participants.

The main goal of the School, following the spirit of the previous schools, was to present to young physicists some actual open problems on various fields of fundamental modern physics. We tried to link the topics belonging to the different fields to a common ground: the coherence in quantum field theories (QED and QCD).

The book contains most of the lectures given at the School in the following fields:
– Coherent phenomena
– Subnuclear physics
– Nuclear physics
– Experimental techniques and particle accelerators

Some papers reflect the tutorial level of the Lecture given at the Course.

We are strongly indebted to Prof. N. Cabibbo, President of the I.N.F.N. for financial support to the School. Acknowledgements are due to Miss L. Bonafini and Mrs. C. Nuncibello for their precious support in organizing the School. Mr. S. Cavallo is acknowledged for his valuable technical assistance.

Thanks are due to the Folgaria Tourism Agency and to the Folgaria Meeting Committee, in particular to Dr. G. Dorigati, Mr. F. Demozzi and Miss A. Ciech for their assistance in the organization.

T. Bressani
B. Minetti
A. Zenoni

Preface

BLDSC *Index of Conference Proceedings*:
    HADRONIC PHYSICS
    1988 Feb   Folgaria, Italy
            Hadronic physics—3rd Winter school—Papers—
            Istituto Nazionale di Fisica Nucleare, Laboratori
            Nazionali di Legnaro
            ISBN 0444874860 U.S.   4237.702 3rd 1988

InterDok:
    2/88-1876 Folgaria, ITA
               Hadronic physics, Winter school 3rd Course
               Ed: Roberto Cherubini, Pietro Dalpiaz, & Bruno Minetti
               Pub: North-Holland Publishing Co.
               Distrib: Elsevier Science Publishers
               US Distrib: Elsevier Science Publishing Co., Inc.
               $110.50   1989 LC89-9473 ISBN 0-444-87486-0

Inspec:
    CONFERENCE PAPER
    Predazzi, E.
            Charm decay and a new hadronization scheme.
    IN: Hadronic Physics, Winter School. (Hadronic Physics. Winter School, Folgaria, Italy, 15-20
    Feb. 1988). Edited by: Cherubini, R.; Dalpiaz, P.; Minetti, B.; Amsterdam, Netherlands:
    North-Holland, 1989. p. 27-37.

Citations to 1988 conference

```
    OCLC:  19670090          Rec stat:    p
    Entered:    19890424     Replaced:    19950514      Used:     19960406
►   Type: a     ELvl:        Srce:        Audn:         Ctrl:        Lang: eng
    BLvl: m     Form:        Conf: 1      Biog:         MRec:        Ctry: ne
                Cont: b      GPub:        Fict: 0       Indx: 1
    Desc: a     Ills: a      Fest: 0      DtSt: s       Dates: 1989,    ¶
►    1  010     89-9473 ¶
►    2  040     DLC ǂc DLC ǂd UKM ¶
►    3  015     GB89-56381 ¶
►    4  019     20723295 ¶
►    5  020     0444874860 (U.S.) ¶
►    6  050 00  QC793.5.H32 ǂb H343 1989 ¶
►    7  082 00  539.7/216 ǂ2 20 ¶
►    8  090     ǂb  ¶
►    9  049     CLUM ¶
►   10  245 00  Hadronic physics : ǂb winter school held at Folgaria, Italy,
    third course, February 15-20, 1988 / ǂc edited by Roberto Cherubini, Pietro
    Dalpiaz, Bruno Minetti. ¶
►   11  260     Amsterdam ; ǂa New York : ǂb North-Holland ; ǂa New York, N.Y.,
    U.S.A. : ǂb Sole distributors for the U.S.A. and Canada, Elsevier Science Pub.
    Co., ǂc 1989. ¶
►   12  300     x, 542 p. : ǂb ill. ; ǂc 25 cm. ¶
►   13  504     Includes bibliographical references and indexes. ¶
►   14  650  0  Hadrons ǂx Congresses. ¶
►   15  650  0  Hadron interactions ǂx Congresses. ¶
►   16  653     Hadrons ǂa Interactions ¶
►   17  700  1  Cherubini, Roberto. ¶
►   18  700  1  Dalpiaz, P. ¶
►   19  700  1  Minetti, Bruno. ¶
```

Bibliographic record for 1988 conference

BLDSC *Index of Conference Proceedings*:

HADRONIC PHYSICS
1991 Feb   Folgaria, Italy
        Common problems and ideas of modern physics--6th
        Winter school on hadronic physics--Papers--
        Istituto Nazionale di Fisica Nucleare, Sezione
        di Torino
        ISBN 9810207115   Common 92/11938

Inspec:

CONFERENCE PAPER
Cicalo, C.; Serci, S.; Usai, G.
        The Mossbauer effect.
IN: Proceedings of the 6th Winter School on Hadronic Physics. Common Problems and Ideas of
Modern Physics, Folgaria, Italy, 4-9 Feb, 1991). Edited by: Bressani, T.; Miretti, B.; Zenoni,
A. Singapore: World Scientific, 1992. p. 87-100.

Citations to 1991 conference

```
  OCLC:   28339410        Rec stat:   a
  Entered:    19930305    Replaced:    19950624    Used:    19960412
▶ Type:   a    ELvl:       Srce:       Audn:       Ctrl:       Lang:  eng
  BLvl:   m    Form:       Conf:  1    Biog:       MRec:       Ctry:  si
               Cont:  b    GPub:       Fict:  0    Indx:  0
  Desc:   a    Ills:  a    Fest:  0    DtSt:  s    Dates: 1992,      ¶
▶   1  010       93-122790 ¶
▶   2  040       DLC ǂc DLC ¶
▶   3  020       9810207115 ¶
▶   4  050 00    QC770 ǂb .W57 1991 ¶
▶   5  082 00    539.7 ǂ2 20 ¶
▶   6  090       ǂb ¶
▶   7  049       CLUM ¶
▶   8  111 2     Winter School on Hadronic Physics ǂn (6th : ǂd 1991 : ǂc
Folgaria, Italy) ¶
▶   9  245 10    Common problems and ideas of modern physics : ǂb proceedings of
the 6th Winter School on Hadronic Physics, Folgaria (Trento), Italy, 4-9
February 1991 / ǂc editors, T. Bressani, B. Minetti, A. Zenoni. ¶
▶  10  260       Singapore ; ǂa River Edge, N.J. : ǂb World Scientific, ǂc
c1992. ¶
▶  11  300       viii, 347 p. : ǂb ill. ; ǂc 23 cm. ¶
▶  12  504       Includes bibliographical references and indexes. ¶
▶  13  650  0    Nuclear physics ǂx Congresses. ¶
▶  14  650  0    Quantum field theory ǂx Congresses. ¶
▶  15  650  0    Coherence (Nuclear physics) ǂx Congresses. ¶
▶  16  700  1    Bressani, Tullio, ǂd 1940- ¶
▶  17  700  1    Minetti, Bruno. ¶
▶  18  700  1    Zenoni, A. ¶
```

Bibliographic record for 1991 conference

Example IV. "ESREF '92"

Exercise:

A. Imagine you are a reference librarian. A patron gives you the following citation, which appears in a list of citations to papers in various sources. How might you search for this in catalogs with which you are familiar?

    [3]   Magistrali, F.; Sala, D.; Tesauri, M.; Fantini, F.:Proc. ESREF 92, Schwäbisch-Gmünd (D), 5-8 October 1992

B. Look at the catalog record for the conference proceedings. Would you have found this record? Why or why not? If you would not have found it, what would have helped you to find it?

Notes:

```
     OCLC:   29638647          Rec stat:    c
     Entered:   19930608·      Replaced:    19950707    Used:   19950709
 ▶ Type:  a       ELvl:        Srce:        Audn:        Ctrl:       Lang:  eng
    BLvl:  m       Form:        Conf:  1     Biog:        MRec:       Ctry:  gw
                   Cont:  b     GPub:        Fict:  0     Indx:  0
     Desc:  a      Ills:  a     Fest:  0     DtSt:  s     Dates:  1992,      ¶
 ▶   1   010       93-163538 ¶
 ▶   2   040       DLC ≠c DLC ¶
 ▶   3   020       3800718863 ¶
 ▶   4   050  00   TK7870 ≠b .E86 1992 ¶
 ▶   5   082  00   621.381 ≠2 20 ¶
 ▶   6   090       ≠b  ¶
 ▶   7   049       CLUM ¶
 ▶   8   111  2    European Symposium on Reliability of Electron Devices, Failure
 Physics, and Analysis ≠n (3rd : ≠d 1992 : ≠c Schw¨abisch Gm¨und, Germany) ¶
 ▶   9   245  10   Conference proceedings / ≠c ESREF 92, 3rd European Symposium on
 Reliability of Electron Devices, Failure Physics and Analysis, Schw¨abisch
 Gm¨und, Germany, 5-8 October 1992 ; conference organizers, ITG,
 Informationstechnische Gesellschaft im VDE in cooperation with GME, VDE-VDI-
 Gesellschaft Mikroelektronik ... [et al.]. ¶
 ▶  10   260       Berlin : ≠b VDE-Verlag, ≠c [c1992] ¶
 ▶  11   300       528 p. : ≠b ill. ; ≠c 30 cm. ¶
 ▶  12   504       Includes bibliographical references. ¶
 ▶  13   650  0    Electronic apparatus and appliances ≠x Reliability ≠x
 Congresses. ¶
 ▶  14   650  0    Electronic apparatus and appliances ≠x Testing ≠x Congresses. ¶
 ▶  15   650  0    Integrated circuits ≠x Reliability ≠x Congresses. ¶
 ▶  16   650  0    Integrated circuits ≠x Testing ≠x Congresses. ¶
 ▶  17   710  2    Informationstechnische Gesellschaft im VDE. ¶
```

Bibliographic record

```
   ARN:    3514672
   Rec stat: n        Entered:      19931214
 ▶ Type:       z       Upd status: a      Enc lvl:   n      Source:
   Roman:      ■       Ref status: a      Mod rec:          Name use: a
   Govt agn:   ■       Auth status: a     Subj:      a      Subj use: a
   Series:     n       Auth/ref:   a      Geo subd:  n      Ser use:  b
   Ser num:    n       Name:       n      Subdiv tp:        Rules:    c ¶
 ▶   1   010       n  93121083  ¶
 ▶   2   040       DLC ≠c DLC ¶
 ▶   3   005       19931214141022.9 ¶
 ▶   4   111  20   European Symposium on Reliability of Electron Devices, Failure
 Physics and Analysis ¶
 ▶   5   411  20   Symposium on Reliability of Electron Devices, Failure Physics
 and Analysis, European ¶
 ▶   6   411  20   ESREF ¶
 ▶   7   670       Conference proceedings, c1992: ≠b t.p. (ESREF 92; 3rd European
 Symposium on Reliability of Electron Devices, Failure Physics and Analysis,
 Schw¨abisch Gm¨und, Germany, 5-8 Oct. 1992) ¶
```

Authority record

CONFERENCE PROCEEDINGS

ESREF 92

3rd EUROPEAN SYMPOSIUM ON RELIABILITY OF ELECTRON DEVICES, FAILURE PHYSICS AND ANALYSIS

Schwäbisch Gmünd, Germany
5–8 October 1992

CONFERENCE ORGANIZERS
ITG Informationstechnische Gesellschaft im VDE

in co-operation with

GME   VDE/VDI-Gesellschaft Mikroelektronik

IEEE   Institute of Electrical and Electronics Engineers (IEEE Region 8, including German Section IEEE)

EUREL   Convention of National Societies of Electrical Engineers of Western Europe

CEC   The Commission of European Communities, ESPRIT Microelectronics Project

CECC   CENELEC Electronic Components Committee

SEE   Société des Electriciens et Electroniciens, France

IQA   Institute for Quality Assurance, United Kingdom

AEI/CCTE   Associazione Elettrotecnica e Elettronica Italia Circuiti Componente Technologia Elettroniche

vde-verlag · Berlin · Offenbach

Title page

Example V. "Crypto '88"

Exercise:

As a cataloger, use the title page, the page facing the t.p. verso, and the foreword, to answer the following questions:

A. Is this the proceedings of a named conference?

B. If so, what is the name and would you make any cross references to that name?

C. What is the main entry for this item?

D. What access points (other than the main entry) would you make to this item?

E. Would you consider cataloging this as a serial rather than as a monograph? Why or why not?

Notes:

Lecture Notes in Computer Science

Edited by G. Goos and J. Hartmanis

403

S. Goldwasser (Ed.)

Advances in Cryptology – CRYPTO '88

Proceedings

Springer-Verlag

Berlin Heidelberg New York London Paris Tokyo Hong Kong

Title page

Title page verso: © Springer—Verlag Berlin Heidelberg 1990

CRYPTO '88

A Conference on the Theory and Application of Cryptography

held at the University of California, Santa Barbara,

August 21-25, 1988

through the cooperation of the Computer Science Department

Sponsored by:

International Association for Cryptologic Research

in cooperation with

The IEEE Computer Society Technical Committee
On Security and Privacy

General Chair
Harold Fredricksen, Naval Postgraduate School

Program Chair
Shafi Goldwasser, Massachusetts Institute of Technology

Program Committee

Eric Bach	University of Wisconsin
Paul Barret	Computer Security Ltd.
Tom Berson	Anagram Laboratories
Gilles Brassard	University of Montreal
Oded Goldreich	Technion Israel Institute of Technology
Andrew Odlyzko	Bell Laboratories
Charles Rackoff	University of Toronto
Ron Rivest	Massachusetts Institute of Technology

Page facing title page verso

Foreword

The papers in this volume were presented at the CRYPTO '88 conference on theory and applications of cryptography, held August 21-25, 1988 in Santa Barbara, California. The conference was sponsored by the International Association for Cryptologic Research (IACR) and hosted by the computer science department at the University of California at Santa Barbara.

The 44 papers presented here comprise: 35 papers selected from 61 extended abstracts submitted in response to the call for papers, 4 invited presentations, and 6 papers selected from a large number of informal rump session presentations.

The papers were chosen by the program committee on the basis of the perceived originality, quality and relevance to the field of cryptography of the extended abstracts submitted. The submissions were not otherwise refereed, and often represent preliminary reports on continuing research.

It is a pleasure to thank many colleagues. Harold Fredricksen singlehandedly made CRYPTO '88 a successful reality. Eric Bach, Paul Barret, Tom Berson, Gilles Brassard, Oded Goldreich, Andrew Odlyzko, Charles Rackoff and Ron Rivest did excellent work on the program committee in putting the technical program together, assisted by kind outside reviewers.

Dawn Crowel at MIT did a super job in publicizing the conference and coordinating the activities of the committee, and Deborah Grupp has been most helpful in the production of this volume. Special thanks are due to Joe Kilian whose humor while assisting me to divide the papers into sessions was indispensable.

Finally, I wish to thank the authors who submitted papers for consideration and the attendants of CRYPTO '88 for their continuing support.

June 1989   Shafi Goldwasser
Cambridge, MA

Foreword

```
OCLC:  20933886           Rec stat:    c
Entered:   19891227·      Replaced:    19950603      Used:    19960406
Type:  a      ELvl:  J    Srce:        Audn:        Ctrl:        Lang:  eng
BLvl:  m      Form:       Conf:  1     Biog:        MRec:        Ctry:  gw
              Cont:  b    GPub:        Fict:  0     Indx:  1
Desc:  a      Ills:  a    Fest:  0     DtSt:  s     Dates: 1990,        ¶
  1   010      89-26359//r90 ¶
  2   040      DLC ≠c DLC ¶
  3   020      0387971963 (U.S. : alk. paper) ¶
  4   050 00   QA76.9.A25 ≠b C79 1988 ¶
  5   082 00   005.8 ≠2 20 ¶
  6   090      ≠b  ¶
  7   049      CLUM ¶
  8   111 2    CRYPTO '88 ≠d (1988 : ≠c University of California, Santa
Barbara) ¶
  9   245 10   Advances in cryptology--CRYPTO '88 : ≠b proceedings / ≠c S.
Goldwasser (ed.). ¶
  10  260      Berlin ; ≠a New York : ≠b Springer-Verlag, ≠c c1990. ¶
  11  300      xi, 591 p. : ≠b ill. ; ≠c 24 cm. ¶
  12  440 0    Lecture notes in computer science ; ≠v 403 ¶
  13  504      Includes bibliographical references and index. ¶
  14  650 0    Computer security ≠x Congresses. ¶
  15  650 0    Cryptography ≠x Congresses. ¶
  16  700 1    Goldwasser, S. ≠q (Shafi), ≠d 1958- ¶
```

Bibliographic record

```
ARN:   877642
Rec stat: c      Entered:      19830407
Type:      z     Upd status:  a     Enc lvl:   n     Source:
Roman:     ■     Ref status:  a     Mod rec:         Name use: a
Govt agn:  ■     Auth status: a     Subj:      a     Subj use: a
Series:    n     Auth/ref:    a     Geo subd:  n     Ser use:  b
Ser num:   n     Name:        n     Subdiv tp:       Rules:    c ¶
  1   010      n 82220908 ≠z n  82260616 ≠z n  85057881 ≠z n  85374479 ≠z n
87891821 ≠z n  88659457 ≠z n  89672116 ≠z n  90628322 ≠z n  91082095 ≠z n
92000213 ≠z n  93090234 ≠z n  94001145 ¶
  2   040      DLC ≠c DLC ≠d DLC ≠d DLC-S ≠d DLC ≠d NjP ¶
  3   005      19941017152213.8 ¶
  4   111 20   CRYPTO ¶
  5   411 20   International Cryptology Conference ¶
  6   670      Its Advances in cryptology, 82: ≠b t.p. (CRYPTO) verso of t.p.
(Proceedings of a workshop on the theory and application of cryptographic
techniques; held at the Univ. of Calif., Santa Barbara) ¶
  7   670      Advances in cryptology, Crypto '94, c1994: ≠b t.p. (14th Annual
International Cryptology Conference, CRYPTO '94, Santa Barbara, Calif., USA,
August 21-25, 1994) ¶
```

Authority record

Citations:

19/88-2466   **Santa Barbara, CA, USA**
CRYPTO, '88 Conf.
Sp: University of California, Santa Barbara
Ti: Advances in Cryptology
(Lecture notes in computer science: ISSN 0302-9743, Vol. 403)
Ed: Shafi Goldwasser
Pub: Springer-Verlag
$42.00 1989 LC89-26359 ISBN 0-387-97196-3

InterDok

1988 Aug   Santa Barbara, CA
Advances in cryptology--Conference on the theory and
application of cryptography--Papers--International
Association for Cryptologic Research--Institute of
Electrical and Electronics Engineers, Computer
Society Technical Committee on Security and Privacy--
[Also known as CRYPTO 88]
ISBN 0387971963 pbk. 3540971963
           5180.185 no 403 1990

BLDSC *Index of Conference Proceedings*

Search request: FIN AU BENALOH, J
Search result: 1 citation in the INSPEC database

To display ABSTRACT, type D <record number> ABS
Type Help for other display options.

1.   CONFERENCE PAPER
    Benaloh, J.; Leichter, J.
     Generalized secret sharing and monotone functions.
    IN: Advances in Cryptology — CRYPTO '88. Proceedings. (Advances in Cryptology
    — CRYPTO '88. Proceedings, Santa Barbara, CA, USA, 21-25 Aug, 1988). Edited
    by: Goldwasser, S. Berlin, West Germany: Springer—Verlag, 1990. p. 27-35.
     Abstract available.
     Pub type: Theoretical or Mathematical.

INSPEC

Example VI. "World marina 91"

Exercise:

As a cataloger, use the title page and the preface to answer the following questions:

A. Is this the proceedings of a named conference?

B. If so, what is the name and would you make any cross references to that name?

C. What is the main entry for this item?

D. What access points (other than the main entry) would you make to this item?

Notes:

WORLD MARINA '91

PROCEEDINGS OF THE FIRST INTERNATIONAL CONFERENCE

Sponsored by the
American Society of Civil Engineers
and the
Southern California Advisory Group

in cooperation with

ALMAR Ltd.
Baker & McKenzie
California Department of Boating and
  Waterways
California Marine Affairs & Navigation
  Conference
California Marine Parks & Harbors
  Association
China Civil Engineering Society
Chinese Institute of Civil and Hydraulic
  Engineering
County of Los Angeles Department of
  Beaches & Harbors
Danish Society of Civil Engineers
Hungarian Federation of Technological
  and Scientific Societies—Scientific
  Society for Building
Illinois Department of Conservation—
  North Point Marina
International Marina Institute
Japan Society of Civil Engineers
Marina & Recreation Association
National Marine Manufacturers
  Association
Noble Consultants, Inc.
Norwegian Society of Chartered
  Engineers
Orange County Environmental
  Management Agency
Parks & Recreation Department, Marine
  Bureau

Permanent International Association of
  Navigation Congresses
Permanent International Association of
  Navigation Congresses—US Section
Société des Ingenieurs et Scientifiques
  de France
Southern California Marine Association
Svenska Vag-Och Vattenbyg_gares
  Riksforbund—(Sweden)
The Association of Finnish Civil
  Engineers
The Canadian Society for Civil Engineering
The Corough Consulting Group
The Hong Kong Institution of Engineers
The Institution of Civil Engineers, UK
The Institution of Engineers, Australia
The Institution of Engineers of Ireland
The Institution of Engineers, Malaysia
The Institution of Engineers, Sri Lanka
The Institution of Engineers, Tanzania
The Institute of Professional Engineers,
  New Zealand
The Institution of Structural Engineers,
  UK
United Design Associates
United States Department of Commerce,
  National Oceanic & Atmospheric
  Administration
University of Wisconsin—Sea Grant
  Institute
US Army Corps of Engineers—
  Waterways Experiment Station

September 4-8, 1991
Long Beach, California

Published by the
American Society of Civil Engineers
345 East 47th Street
New York, New York 10017-2398

Title page

PREFACE

The World Marina '91 Conference is a specialty conference addressed to the operation and development of harbors and boating facilities associated with the needs of recreational boating. Sport and pleasure navigation activities continue to increase in popularity throughout the world. Development of quality marina facilities and operation management are important factors in this continuing growth. As with other uses of coastal and waterside resources, the need for recreational boating facilities to consider overall environmental factors and constraints is becoming increasingly more important. The considerations of water quality, marine habitat protection and mitigation, along with local social and economic needs, can be significant factors in developing boater support facilities. Technologies and economic options for the mid-size boat owners are creating opportunities for alternate concepts of boat handling and storage. The conference papers address many of these factors from a variety of viewpoints, along with case studies of marina development experiences throughout the world. It is a privilege to hold this conference in the Southern California area, which is now entering its fifth decade of modern marina development.

The conference has been, in part, inspired by the International Marina Conference held in Brisbane, Australia in 1987, whose concept and organization were initiated by local Brisbane marina interests. We are indebted to Mr. Bob Hope of Brisbane for his early advice and encouragement. The local Southern California advisory group was formed with participants from all phases of the area's marina and development interests. This local group, combined with the overall direction and sponsorship of the American Society of Civil Engineers, has resulted in the conference and these proceedings. We thank the authors for their contributions.

Local Advisory Committee Members

Victor Adorian, Chairman, Past Director, Dept. of Beaches and Harbors,
  County of Los Angeles

Ted Reed, Current Director, Dept. of Beaches and Harbors, County of Los Angeles
Robert F. Wingard, Director, Environmental Management Agency, Orange County
Harry L. Nelson, Jr., President, ALMAR Ltd.
Richard L. Miller, Director, Marine Bureau, City of Long Beach
Lawrence E. Williams, Principal, Williams-Kuebelbeck and Associates
John C. Corough, President, The Corough Group
Gordon R. Fulton, President, Concept Marine Corporation
Ronald Noble, President, Noble Consultants, Inc.
James R. Walker, Vice President, Moffat & Nichol, Engineers
John M. Nichol, Consulting Engineer

iii

Preface-p. iii

WORLD MARINA
1991 Sep   Long Beach, CA
    World marina '91 - 1st International conference -
Papers - American Society of Civil Engineers
ISBN 0872628426 pbk.   9356.55887 1991

BLDSC Index of Conference Proceedings citation

9/91-0799   **Long Beach, CA, USA**
    World marina '91, 1st intl. conf.
    Sp: American Society of Civil Engineers (ASCE)
    Pub: American Society of Civil Engineers
    $68.00   1991 LC91-25770 ISBN 0-87262-842-6 764p.

InterDok citation

03352730   E.I. Monthly No: EIM9112-064414
    Title: Innovation in the marina facilities.
    Author: Matsumoto, Takeji; Mukaidani, Mitoku; Ishii, Motaetsu
    Corporate Source: Steel Structures Dept
    Conference Title: Proceedings of the First International Conference on
    World Marina '91
    Location: Long Beach, CA, USA   Conference Date: 1991 Sep 4-8
    E.I. Conference No.: 15178
    Source: Proc First Int Conf World Mar 91. Publ by ASCE, New York, NY,
    USA, p. 716-724
    Publication Year: 1991
    ISBN: 0-87262-842-6
    Language: English

COMPENDEX citation

```
  OCLC:   24142057              Rec stat:      p
  Entered:      19910621        Replaced:      19950430        Used:      19960408
▶ Type:  a      ELvl:        Srce:       Audn:       Ctrl:        Lang:   eng
  BLvl:  m      Form:        Conf:  1    Biog:       MRec:        Ctry:   nyu
               Cont:   b     GPub:       Fict:  0    Indx:  1
  Desc:  a      Ills:  ab    Fest:  0    DtSt:  s    Dates: 1991,        ¶
▶  1   010      91-25770 ¶
▶  2   040      DLC ǂc DLC ¶
▶  3   020      0872628426 ¶
▶  4   050 00   VK369 ǂb .W67 1991 ¶
▶  5   082 00   627/.38 ǂ2 20 ¶
▶  6   090      ǂb  ¶
▶  7   049      CLUM ¶
▶  8   245 00   World marina '91 : ǂb proceedings of the first international
conference / ǂc sponsored by the American Society of Civil Engineers and the
Southern California advisory group in cooperation with ALMAR Ltd. ... [et
al.]. ¶
▶  9   260      New York, N.Y. : ǂb The Society, ǂc c1991. ¶
▶ 10   300      x, 764 p. : ǂb ill., maps ; ǂc 22 cm. ¶
▶ 11   500      "September 4-8, 1991, Long Beach, California." ¶
▶ 12   504      Includes bibliographical references and index. ¶
▶ 13   650   0  Marinas ǂx Congresses. ¶
▶ 14   710 2    American Society of Civil Engineers. ¶
```

Bibliographic record (record altered; may not match OCLC version)

Example VII. "Compcon"

Exercise:

On the next page, the verso of the first leaf of this item and the recto of the second leaf (p. [ii] and [iii]) are reproduced. As a cataloger of this item

A. Select a chief source of information.

B. Determine the title proper, other title information (if any) and statement of responsibility for this item.

C. Would you make any notes (500 fields) on the record for this item? If so, what note(s) would you make (aside from a bibliography note)?

D. Determine whether the conference is named, what its name is if it has a name, and what cross references you would make to such a name (you may want to use the reproduction of p. v, in addition to the other pages, to answer this question)

E. Determine the main entry and any added entries that you would make to this item.

F. Would you consider cataloging this as a serial rather than as a monograph? Why or why not?

Notes:

COMPCON SPRING '91

digest of papers

San Francisco, California
February 25 - March 1, 1991

IEEE Computer Society Press
Los Alamitos, California

Washington • Brussels • Tokyo

p. [iii]

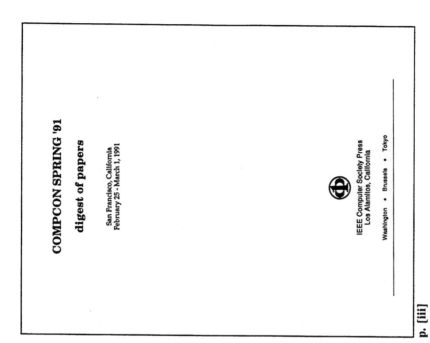

p. [ii]

General Chairman's Message

Welcome to San Francisco and the Cathedral Hill Hotel for the 36th Annual IEEE International Computer Conference, COMPCON Spring '91. The nature of COMPCON, this year's only broad-based general computer conference sponsored by the IEEE Computer Society, demands a good balance between depth and breadth in coverage of computer-related topics. We continue the conference format started three years ago, offering special featured sessions at the beginning of each day of the technical program to hear personal insights from industry leaders, followed by four parallel tracks, each on a special theme. The conference also has seven tutorial sessions, four on Monday and three on Friday.

The production of COMPCON is made possible by the collective effort of many volunteers, especially the members of the Steering Committee headed by Fred Buelow, and several subcommittes. Many thanks are due to Glen Langdon, Jim Dickie, Bob Fink, Andy Goforth, Rex Rice and Pam Sloan for their enormous and meticulous effort in running the publicity campaign for this year's COMPCON. Special thanks to Bob Fink for his effort and dedication in setting up the local arrangements, and to Roy Lee and Joe Fernandez for organizing the Monday and Friday tutorials. We also thank Dave Hunt, Ross Gaunt, Lori Goerz, Donna Hunt and Jim Rawlings for their administrative support in handling registration and the treasury. Jackie Olila deserves a special recognition for her perseverance and effort in putting together this Digest of Papers. We are also grateful to the members of the IEEE Computer Society's local chapter for their contributions, especially their liaison on our Steering Committee, Ken Majithia. Last, but not least, we thank Ken Miura and Sid Fernbach for their continued advice and guidance to this year's committee.

The heart of COMPCON is the technical program. This is the result of the planning, patience and hard work of our Program Co-Chairs, Michelle Aden and Creve Maples and the contributions of the distinguished members of their Program Committee. We are sure that the result of their effort is an excellent program covering a wide range of topics in the computer field. We also appreciate the effort put forth by the individual session chairpeople and all of the speakers in the conference.

We would like to bring to your attention the two social hours on Tuesday and Wednesday at 5 P.M. There you will have the opportunity to meet your fellow attendees and to meet and discuss the conference with the members of the various COMPCON committees. The entire production committees wish you an enjoyable week at COMPCON under our continued Intellectual Leverage theme!

Roger E. Anderson
General Chairman
COMPCON Spring '91

v

```
     OCLC:  25985342          Rec stat:    a
     Entered:    19901102     Replaced:    19950529      Used:    19950610
  ▶ Type:  a     ELvl:        Srce:        Audn:         Ctrl:        Lang:  eng
     BLvl:  m     Form:        Conf:  1     Biog:         MRec:        Ctry:  cau
                  Cont:  b     GPub:        Fict:  0      Indx:  1
     Desc:  a     Ills:  a     Fest:  0     DtSt:  s      Dates: 1991,     ¶
  ▶  1   010     90-85549 ¶
  ▶  2   040     DLC ≠c DLC ¶
  ▶  3   020     0818621346 ¶
  ▶  4   020     0818661348 (microfiche) ¶
  ▶  5   020     0818691344 (case) ¶
  ▶  6   050 00  QA75.5 ≠b .C58 1991 ¶
  ▶  7   082 00  004 ≠2 20 ¶
  ▶  8   090     ≠b  ¶
  ▶  9   049     CLUM ¶
  ▶ 10   111 2   Compcon ≠n (36th : ≠d 1991 : ≠c San Francisco, Calif.) ¶
  ▶ 11   245 00  Digest of papers / ≠c Compcon spring '91, San Francisco,
  California, February 25-March 1, 1991. ¶
  ▶ 12   260     Los Alamitos, Calif. : ≠b IEEE Computer Society Press, ≠c
  c1991. ¶
  ▶ 13   300     xiv, 599 p. : ≠b ill. ; ≠c 28 cm. ¶
  ▶ 14   500     "Intellectual leverage"--P. facing t.p. ¶
  ▶ 15   504     Includes bibliographical references and index. ¶
  ▶ 16   650 0   Computers ≠x Congresses. ¶
  ▶ 17   710 2   IEEE Computer Society. ¶
  ▶ 18   740 01  Intellectual leverage. ¶
```

Bibliographic record (record altered; may not match OCLC version)

```
      ARN:    374322
      Rec stat: c        Entered:      19800307
   ▶ Type:     z         Upd status:  a     Enc lvl:   n      Source:
      Roman:    ■         Ref status:  a     Mod rec:          Name use: a
      Govt agn: ■         Auth status: a     Subj:      a      Subj use: a
      Series:   n         Auth/ref:    a     Geo subd:  n      Ser use:  b
      Ser num:  n         Name:        n     Subdiv tp: ■      Rules:    c ¶
   ▶   1   010      n  79143121 ≠z n  84199271  ¶
   ▶   2   040      DLC ≠c DLC ≠d DLC ¶
   ▶   3   005      19891010113533.9 ¶
   ▶   4   111 20   Compcon. ¶
   ▶   5   411 20   IEEE Computer Society International Conference ¶
   ▶   6   411 20   IEEE International Computer Conference ¶
   ▶   7   511 20   Computer Group Conference ≠w nnnd ¶
   ▶   8   511 20   IEEE Computer Conference ≠w nnnd ¶
   ▶   9   511 20   Fall Joint Computer Conference ≠w b ¶
   ▶  10   665      Publications of this series of meetings are found under the
   following headings: ≠a 1st: IEEE Computer Conference, 1st, Chicago, 1967. ≠a
   2d: Computer Group Conference, 2d, Los Angeles, 1968. ≠a 3d: Computer Group
   Conference, 3d, Minneapolis, 1969. ≠a 6th: Compcon. ≠a SUBJECT ENTRY: Works
   about this conference are entered under the name used at the time of the
   publication. ¶
   ▶  11   670      Its 6th, San Francisco, 1972. Digest of papers, 1972. ¶
   ▶  12   670      Its (30th : 1985 : San Francisco, Calif.). Technological
   leverage, a competitive necessity, c1985: ≠b t.p. (Compcon 85; Thirtieth IEEE
   Computer Society International Conference ¶
   ▶  13   670      Fall Joint Computer Conference (1st : 1986 : Dallas, Tex.). 1986
   proceedings, c1986: ≠b t.p. (Fall Joint Computer Conference) p. xxi (the ACM
   National Conference and the COMPCON fall meeting of the Computer Society of the
   IEEE combined to form the Fall Joint Computer Conference) ¶
   ▶  14   670      Its (36th : 1991 : San Francisco, Calif.). Digest of papers,
   c1991: ≠b t.p. (Compcon spring '91) p. v (IEEE International Computer
   Conference) ¶
```

Authority record (record altered; may not match OCLC version)

CONFERENCE PAPER

Dorr, M. R.; Ferguson, J. M.
A killer micro attack on 3D neutron transport.
IN: COMPCON Spring '91. Digest of Papers (Cat. No. 91CH2961-1). (COMPCON
Spring '91. Digest of papers (Cat. No. 91CH296-1), San Francisco, CA, USA,
25 Feb.-1 March 1991). Los Alamitos, CA, USA: IEEE Comput. Soc. Press, 1991.
p. 51-6.

Citation from INSPEC

COMPCON
1991 Feb ·   San Francisco, CA
Intellectual leverage -- 36th International conference -- Papers -- Institute of
Electrical and Electronics Engineers. Computer Society-[100 Papers, Also
known as COMPCON Spring '91. IEEE cat. no. 91CH2961-1]
ISBN 0818621346 paper, 081661348 microfiche, 0818691344 case 3363.922 1991

Citation from BLDSC *Index of Conference Proceedings*

2/91-01-0121   San Francisco, CA, USA
           Computer conf., IEEE Computer Society 36th Spring Intl. conf.
           (COMPCON)(Intellectual leverage)
           Sp: IEEE Computer Society
           Sp: Institute of Electrical & Electronics Engineers (IEEE)
           Pub: IEEE Computer Society Press
                (IEEE Computer Society order no. 2134)
           Pub: IEEE
                (IEEE cat. no. 91CH2961-1)
           $90.00 1991 LC90-85549 ISBN 0-8186-2134-6 599p.

Citation from InterDok

003386035 E.I. Monthly No: EIM9202-010430
Title: A killer micro attack on 3D neutron transport.
Author: Dorr, Milo R.; Ferguson, James M.
Corporate Source: Lawrence Livermore Nat Lab, Livermore, CA, USA
Conference Title: 36th IEEE Computer Society International Conference -
COMPCON Spring '91 Conference. Location: San Francisco, CA, USA Conference.
Date: 1991 Feb 25-Mar 1. E.I. Conference No.: 15855. Source: Digest of
Papers - IEEE Computer Society International Conference. Publ. by IEEE
Service Center, Piscataway, NJ, USA (IEEE cat n 91CH2961-1). p.51-56.
Publication Year: 1991. CODEN: DCSIDU. ISBN: 0-81862134-6.

Citation from COMPENDEX

Example VIII. "IAU/International Astronomical Union Colloquium"

Exercise:

As a cataloger, use the title page of each of these two proceedings, as well as the authority records provided, to answer the following questions:

A. What is the name of the conference?

      April 1989 colloquium:

      August 1989 colloquium:

B. What access points would you provide in addition to the name of the conference?

      April 1989 colloquium:

      August 1989 colloquium:

Notes:

Lecture Notes in Physics

Edited by H. Araki, Kyoto, J. Ehlers, München, K. Hepp, Zürich
R. Kippenhahn, München, D. Ruelle, Bures-sur-Yvette
H. A. Weidenmüller, Heidelberg, J. Wess, Karlsruhe and J. Zittartz, Köln

Managing Editor: W. Beiglböck

350

G. Tenorio-Tagle   M. Moles
J. Melnick (Eds.)

Structure and Dynamics of the Interstellar Medium

Proceedings of IAU Colloquium No. 120
Held on the Occasion of Guido's Jubilee
in Granada, Spain, April 17–21, 1989

Springer-Verlag

Berlin Heidelberg New York London Paris Tokyo Hong Kong

April 1989 Colloquium--Title page

LIGHT POLLUTION, RADIO INTERFERENCE,
AND SPACE DEBRIS

Proceedings of the International Astronomical Union
Colloquium No. 112, held 13 to 16 August 1989
in Washington, DC

August 1989 Colloquium--Title page

ASTRONOMICAL SOCIETY OF THE PACIFIC
CONFERENCE SERIES

Volume 17

LIGHT POLLUTION, RADIO INTERFERENCE,
AND SPACE DEBRIS

Edited By

DAVID L. CRAWFORD

August 1989 Colloquium--Series title page

```
    ARN:   1103310
    Rec stat: c        Entered:      19840409
▶ Type:      z        Upd status: a    Enc lvl:  n     Source:
    Roman:    ▉        Ref status: a    Mod rec:        Name use: a
    Govt agn: ▉        Auth status: a   Subj:     a     Subj use: a
    Series:   n        Auth/ref:   a    Geo subd: n     Ser use:  b
    Ser num:  n        Name:       n    Subdiv tp:      Rules:    c ¶
▶  1  010     n 84007626 ≠z n 79088033  ¶
▶  2  040     DLC ≠c DLC ≠d DLC ¶
▶  3  005     19941121100453.2 ¶
▶  4  111 20  IAU Colloquium ¶
▶  5  411 20  I.A.U. Colloquium ¶
▶  6  411 20  Colloque de l'U.A.I. ¶
▶  7  411 20  Colloque de l'UAI ¶
▶  8  510 20  International Astronomical Union. ≠b Colloquium ¶
▶  9  667     Heading valid for meetings with the name "IAU Colloquium [no.]".
For meetings with the name "[no.] Colloquium of the International Astronomical
Union" and "International Astronomical Union Colloquium [no.]," use the
heading: International Astronomical Union. Colloquium ... Both headings are
valid since the name fluctuates from meeting to meeting ¶
▶ 10  670     Its (10th : 1970 : Cambridge, Cambridgeshire). Gravitational N-
body problem, 1972: ≠b t.p. (IAU Colloquium no. 10, Cambridge, England, 8/12-
15/70) ¶
▶ 11  670     Its (17th : 1972 : Observatoire de Paris-Meudon). Age des ̄
¯etoiles, 1972?: ≠b t.p. (Colloque no. 17 de l'U.A.I.) ¶
▶ 12  675     Int. Astronom. Union. Coll. (1st : Astronomical Observatory,
National University of La Plata). The problem of the variation of the
geographical ... 1972: t.p. (Colloquium no. 1 of the International Astronomical
Union); ≠a Int. Astronom. Union. Coll. (11th : 1970 : Edinburgh, Lothian).
Automation in optical ... 1971: t.p. (Colloquium no. 11 of the International
Astronomical Union) ¶
```

Authority record

```
    ARN:   712815
    Rec stat: c        Entered:      19820211
▶ Type:      z        Upd status: a    Enc lvl:  n     Source:
    Roman:    ▉        Ref status: a    Mod rec:        Name use: a
    Govt agn: ▉        Auth status: a   Subj:     a     Subj use: a
    Series:   n        Auth/ref:   a    Geo subd: n     Ser use:  b
    Ser num:  n        Name:       n    Subdiv tp:      Rules:    c ¶
▶  1  010     n 82015565 ≠z n 77016941  ¶
▶  2  040     DLC ≠c DLC ≠d DLC ¶
▶  3  005     19940511104609.3 ¶
▶  4  110 20  International Astronomical Union. ≠b Colloquium ¶
▶  5  410 20  International Astronomical Union. ≠b Colloque ¶
▶  6  411 20  Colloquium of the International Astronomical Union ¶
▶  7  511 20  IAU Colloquium ¶
▶  8  667     Heading valid for meetings with the name "[no.] Colloquium of
the International Astronomical Union" and "International Astronomical Union
Colloquium [no.]." For meetings with the name "IAU Colloquium [no.]," use the
heading: IAU Colloquium ... Both headings are valid since the name fluctuates
from meeting to meeting ¶
▶  9  670     Its (56th : 1980 : Warsaw, Poland). Reference coordinate systems
for earth dynamics, c1981: ≠b t.p. (56th Colloquium of the International
Astronomical Union held in Warsaw, Poland, 9/8-12/80) ¶
▶ 10  670     Its (37th : 1976 : Paris, France). D' ̄ecalages vers le rouge ...
1977: ≠b t.p. (Colloque de l'Union astronomique internationale no 37) ¶
▶ 11  675     IAU Coll. (49th : 1978 : Groningen, Netherlands). Image
formation ... c1979: t.p. (IAU Colloquium); ≠a IAU Coll. (59th : 1980 :
Trieste, Italy). Effects of mass ... c1981: t.p. (IAU Colloquium no. 59) ¶
```

Authority record

```
     OCLC:  20629063        Rec stat:    c
     Entered:    19891023       Replaced:    19950530      Used:    19960420
  ▶ Type:  a     ELvl:       Srce:        Audn:        Ctrl:        Lang: eng
     BLvl:  m     Form:       Conf:  1     Biog:        MRec:        Ctry: gw
                  Cont:  b    GPub:        Fict:  0     Indx:  0
     Desc:  a     Ills:  a    Fest:  1     DtSt:  s     Dates: 1989,       ¶
  ▶  1  010        89-29570 ¶
  ▶  2  040        DLC ‡c DLC ¶
  ▶  3  020        0387519564 (U.S. : alk. paper) : ‡c $62.70 (DM116.00 West
Germany) ¶
  ▶  4  050 00    QB790 ‡b .I28 1989 ¶
  ▶  5  082 00    523.1/35 ‡2 20 ¶
  ▶  6  090        ‡b  ¶
  ▶  7  049        CLUM ¶
  ▶  8  111 2      IAU Colloquium ‡n (120th : ‡d 1989 : ‡c Granada, Spain) ¶
  ▶  9  245 10    Structure and dynamics of the interstellar medium : ‡b
proceedings of IAU Colloquium No. 120, held on the occassion of Guido's jubilee
in Granada, Spain, April 17-21, 1989 / ‡c G. Tenorio-Tagle, M. Moles, J.
Melnick (eds.). ¶
  ▶ 10  260        Berlin ; ‡a New York : ‡b Springer-Verlag, ‡c c1989. ¶
  ▶ 11  300        xxi, 537 p. : ‡c ill. 24 cm. ¶
  ▶ 12  440 0      Lecture notes in physics ; ‡v 350 ¶
  ▶ 13  504        Includes bibliographical references. ¶
  ▶ 14  650 0      Interstellar matter ‡x Congresses. ¶
  ▶ 15  650 0      Molecular clouds ‡x Congresses. ¶
  ▶ 16  650 0      Stars ‡x Formation ‡x Congresses. ¶
  ▶ 17  650 0      Galaxies ‡x Congresses. ¶
  ▶ 18  651 0      Orion Nebula ‡x Congresses. ¶
  ▶ 19  600 20    M¨unch Galindo, Guido. ¶
  ▶ 20  700 2      Tenorio-Tagle, G. ‡q (Guillermo), ‡d 1947- ¶
  ▶ 21  700 1      Moles, M. ‡q (Mariano), ‡d 1946- ¶
  ▶ 22  700 1      Melnick, Jorge. ¶
  ▶ 23  710 2      International Astronomical Union. ¶
```

April 1989 Colloquium--Bibliographic record

012.121   **Structure and dynamics of the interstellar medium.**
             Proceedings, IAU Colloquium No. 120 on Guido
        Münch's Jubilee: Structure and dynamics of the interstellar
        medium, Granada (Spain), 17-21 Apr 1989.
        G. Tenorio-Tagle, M. Moles, J. Melnick (eds.).
        Lect. Notes Phys., Vol. 350
        Springer, Berlin (Germany, F.R.). 558 p. (1989). ISBN 3-540-51956-4.
        Price DM 116.00. ISBN 0-387-51956-4 (USA).

April 1989 Colloquium--citation from *Astronomy & Astrophysics Abstracts*

```
     OCLC:  23996076          Rec stat:      a
     Entered:    19910225     Replaced:      19950609      Used:     19960420
▶ Type: a      ELvl:       Srce:       Audn:       Ctrl:        Lang: eng
   BLvl: m      Form:       Conf: 1     Biog:       MRec:        Ctry: cau
                Cont:  b     GPub:       Fict: 0     Indx: 0
   Desc: a      Ills:  a    Fest: 0     DtSt: s     Dates: 1991,     ¶
▶   1  010      91-55139 ¶
▶   2  040      DLC ǂc DLC ¶
▶   3  020      0937707368 ¶
▶   4  050 00   QB476.5 ǂb .I58 1989 ¶
▶   5  082 00   522 ǂ2 20 ¶
▶   6  090      ǂb  ¶
▶   7  049      CLUM ¶
▶   8  110 2    International Astronomical Union. ǂb Colloquium ǂn (112th : ǂd
1989 : ǂc Washington, D.C.) ¶
▶   9  245 10   Light pollution, radio interference, and space debris : ǂb
proceedings of the International Astronomical Union Colloquium no. 112, held 13
to 16 August 1989 in Washington, DC. ¶
▶  10  260      San Francisco, Calif. : ǂb Astronomical Society of the Pacific,
ǂc 1991. ¶
▶  11  300      xiv, 331 p. : ǂb ill. ; ǂc 24 cm. ¶
▶  12  440  0   Astronomical Society of the Pacific conference series ; ǂv v.
17 ¶
▶  13  500      "Edited by David L. Crawford"--Ser. t.p. ¶
▶  14  504      Includes bibliographical references. ¶
▶  15  650  0   Radio astronomy ǂx Observations ǂx Congresses. ¶
▶  16  650  0   Radio ǂx Interference ǂx Congresses. ¶
▶  17  650  0   Light ǂx Environmental aspects ǂx Observations ǂx Congresses. ¶
▶  18  650  0   Space debris ǂx Congresses. ¶
▶  19  700  1   Crawford, David Livingstone, ǂd 1931- ¶
```

August 1989 Colloquium--Bibliographic record

012.121   **Light pollution, radio interference and space debris. IAU
            Colloquium No. 112: Light pollution, radio interference
and space debris**, Washington, DC (USA), 13-16 Aug 1988.
D. L. Crawford (ed.)
Astron. Soc. Pac. Conf. Ser., Vol. 17.
Astronomical Society of the Pacific, San Francisco, CA (USA)
347 p. (1991). ISBN 0-937707-36-8

August 1989 Colloquium--Citation from *Astronomy & Astrophysics Abstracts*

Example IX. "Production, refining ..."

Exercise:

As a cataloger, use the title page and authority records to answer the following questions:

A. What is the main entry for this item?

B. What added entries would you make for this item?

Notes:

PROCEEDINGS OF THE INTERNATIONAL SYMPOSIUM ON
PRODUCTION, REFINING, FABRICATION AND
RECYCLING OF LIGHT METALS
HAMILTON, ONTARIO, AUGUST 26-30, 1990

Production, Refining, Fabrication and Recycling of Light Metals

Editors

Michel Bouchard
Université du Québec à Chicoutimi
Chicoutimi, Québec

Pierre Tremblay
Alcan International Ltée,
Jonquière, Québec

Symposium organized by the Light Metals Section of
The Metallurgical Society of CIM

29th ANNUAL CONFERENCE OF METALLURGISTS OF CIM
29ᵉ CONFÉRENCE ANNUELLE DES MÉTALLURGISTES DE L'ICM

Pergamon Press
Member of Maxwell Macmillan Pergamon Publishing Corporation
New York   Oxford   Beijing   Frankfurt   São Paulo   Sydney   Tokyo   Toronto

Title page

```
    ARN:   2787816
    Rec stat: c       Entered:      19900726
►  Type:      z       Upd status: a      Enc lvl:   n      Source:
    Roman:     ■       Ref status: a      Mod rec:           Name use: a
    Govt agn: ■        Auth status: a     Subj:        a     Subj use: a
    Series:    n       Auth/ref:   a      Geo subd:  n       Ser use:  b
    Ser num:   n       Name:       n      Subdiv tp: ■       Rules:    c ¶
►  1  010     n 90674775 ¶
►  2  040     DLC ≠c DLC ≠d DLC ¶
►  3  005     19900801090559.1 ¶
►  4  111 20  International Symposium on Production, Refining, Fabrication,
and Recycling of Light Metals ≠d (1990 : ≠c Hamilton, Ont.) ¶
►  5  411 20  Symposium on Production, Refining, Fabrication, and Recycling of
Light Metals, International ¶
    6  670     Its Production, refining, fabrication, and recycling ... 1990:
≠b CIP t.p. (International Symposium on Production, Refining, Fabrication, and
Recycling of Light Metals, Hamilton, Ont., 08/26-30/90) ¶
```

Authority record

```
    ARN:   1579168
    Rec stat: c       Entered:      19860508
►  Type:      z       Upd status: a      Enc lvl:   n      Source:
    Roman:     ■       Ref status: a      Mod rec:           Name use: a
    Govt agn: ■        Auth status: a     Subj:        a     Subj use: a
    Series:    n       Auth/ref:   a      Geo subd:  n       Ser use:  b
    Ser num:   n       Name:       n      Subdiv tp: ■       Rules:    c ¶
►  1  010     n 85288379 ¶
►  2  040     DLC ≠c DLC ≠d DLC ≠d NmU ¶
►  3  005     19950812060401.3 ¶
►  4  111 20  Conference of Metallurgists. ¶
►  5  411 20  Conference of Metallurgists of CIM ¶
►  6  411 20  Congr`es des m´etallurgistes de l'ICM ¶
►  7  411 20  Conf´erence des m´etallurgistes ¶
►  8  411 20  Conf´erence des m´etallurgistes de l'ICM ¶
►  9  670     Hydrometallurgical Meeting (15th : 1985 : Vancouver, B.C.).
Impurity control & disposal, 1985: ≠b t.p. (24th annual Conference of
Metallurgists, Vancouver, 8/18-22/85) ¶
► 10  670     NLC, 11-26-85 ≠b (AACR 2: Conference of Metallurgists) ¶
► 11  670     International Symposium on the Production and Processing of Fine
Particles (1988 : Montr´eal, Qu´ebec). Production and processing of fine
particles, 1988: ≠b CIP t.p. (27th Annual Conference of Metallurgists of CIM;
27e Congr`es annuel des m´etallurgistes de l'ICM) ¶
► 12  670     Phone call to NLC, 7-6-88 ≠b (According to contact with Canadian
Institute of Mining and Metallurgy, name of conference hasn't changed; name in
French: Conf´erence des m´etallurgistes) ¶
► 13  670     Impurity control and disposal in hydrometalurgical processes,
c1994: ≠b t.p. (33rd Annual Conference of Metallurgists of CIM; 33e Conf´erence
annuelle des m´etallurgi[s]tes de l'ICM) ¶
```

Authority record

```
    OCLC:   24219246           Rec stat:    n
    Entered:    19900724·      Replaced:    19950502      Used:    19950410
▶  Type:  a     ELvl:  8    Srce:        Audn:        Ctrl:        Lang:  eng
    BLvl:  m     Form:       Conf:  1     Biog:        MRec:        Ctry:  nyu
                 Cont:  b    GPub:        Fict:  0     Indx:  1
    Desc:  a     Ills:       Fest:  0     DtSt:  s     Dates:  1990,      ¶
▶   1  010      90-43192 ¶
▶   2  040      DLC ≠c DLC ¶
▶   3  015      C93-564-3 ¶
▶   4  019      27070108 ¶
▶   5  020      0080404162 ¶
▶   6  050 00   TN775 ≠b .I569 1990 ¶
▶   7  055 0    TN775 ≠b I569 1990 fol. ¶
▶   8  082 00   673/.722 ≠2 20 ¶
▶   9  090      ≠b  ¶
▶  10  049      CLUM ¶
▶  11  111 2    International Symposium on Production, Refining, Fabrication,
   and Recycling of Light Metals ≠d (1990 : ≠c Hamilton, Ont.) ¶
▶  12  245 10   Production, refining, fabrication, and recycling of light metals
   : ≠b proceedings of the International Symposium on Production, Refining,
   Fabrication, and Recycling of Light Metals, Hamilton, Ontario, August 26-30,
   1990 / ≠c editors, Michel Bouchard, Pierre Tremblay. ¶
▶  13  260      New York : ≠b Pergamon Press, ≠c 1990. ¶
▶  14  263      9008 ¶
▶  15  300      361 p. : ≠b ill. ; ≠c 26 cm. ¶
▶  16  490 1    Proceedings / Metallurgical Society of the Canadian Institute of
   Mining and Metallurgy ; ≠v v. 19 ¶
▶  17  500      "Symposium organized by the Light Metals Section of the
   Metallurgical Society of CIM." ¶
▶  18  500      "29th Annual Conference of Metallurgists of CIM; 29e Confˊerence
   annuelle des mˊetallurgistes de L'ICM." ¶
▶  19  504      Includes bibliographical references and indexes. ¶
▶  20  650 0    Aluminum ≠x Metallurgy ≠x Congresses. ¶
▶  21  650 0    Magnesium ≠x Metallurgy ≠x Congresses. ¶
▶  22  650 0    Smelting ≠x Congresses. ¶
▶  23  650 0    Recycling (Waste, etc.) ≠x Congresses. ¶
▶  24  650 6    Mˊetaux lˊegers ≠x Congrˋes. ¶
▶  25  700 1    Bouchard, Michel, ≠d 1942- ¶
▶  26  700 1    Tremblay, Pierre. ¶
▶  27  710 2    Metallurgical Society of CIM. ≠b Light Metals Section. ¶
▶  28  711 2    Conference of Metallurgists ≠n (29th : ≠d 1990 : ≠c Hamilton,
   Ont.) ¶
▶  29  830 0    Proceedings of the Metallurgical Society of the Canadian
   Institute of  Mining and Metallurgy ; ≠v vol. 19. ¶
```

Bibliographic record

1990 Aug	Hamilton. Canada

Production, refining, fabrication and recycling of light metals -- International symposium -- 29th Annual conference of metallurgists -- Papers -- Canadian Institute of Mining and Metallurgy, Metallurgical Society, Light Metals Section -- [33 Papers]

ISBN 0080404162   1082.436 vol 19 1990

Citation from BLDSC Index of Conference Proceedings

Example X. "Cryptography and coding"

Exercise:

As a reference librarian, you are given the following citation by a patron.

> [4]   A. Beutelspacher and K. Vedder, "Geometric Structures as Threshold Schemes," <u>Proceedings of the 1987 IMA Conference on Cryptography and Coding Theory</u>, Cirencester, England, Oxford University Press, to appear.

In catalogs with which you are familiar, how would you search for the published proceedings? List as many possibilities as you can think of.

Now, look at the bibliographic record for the proceedings. Would you have retrieved this record with any of your searches? If you would have, would you have recognized it as the record you were seeking? (It <u>is</u> the correct record.)

Finally, look at the title page and preface of the item. Is there information here that would have helped you to identify the item if it had been used in the bibliographic record?

Notes:

```
        OCLC:  19555283        Rec stat:      c
        Entered:    19890327    Replaced:    19950513     Used:    19960515
    ▶ Type:  a     ELvl:      Srce:      Audn:       Ctrl:       Lang:  eng
        BLvl:  m     Form:      Conf:  1   Biog:       MRec:       Ctry:  enk
                     Cont:  b   GPub:      Fict:  0    Indx:  0
        Desc:  a     Ills:  a   Fest:  0   DtSt:  s    Dates: 1989,    ¶
    ▶   1  010     89-3429 ¶
    ▶   2  040     DLC ‡c DLC ¶
    ▶   3  020     0198536232 : ‡c £35.00 ($52.00 U.S.) ¶
    ▶   4  050 00  QA268 ‡b .C74 1989 ¶
    ▶   5  082 00  003/.54 ‡2 20 ¶
    ▶   6  090     ‡b ¶
    ▶   7  049     CLUM ¶
    ▶   8  245 00  Cryptography and coding / ‡c edited by Henry J. Beker and F.C.
    Piper. ¶
    ▶   9  260     Oxford : ‡b Clarendon Press ; ‡a New York : ‡b Oxford University
    Press, ‡c 1989. ¶
    ▶  10  300     x, 297 p. : ‡b ill. ; ‡c 25 cm. ¶
    ▶  11  440  4  The Institute of Mathematics and its Applications conference
    series ; ‡v new ser., 20 ¶
    ▶  12  500     "Based on the proceedings of a conference organized by the
    Institute of Mathematics and its Applications on cryptography and coding, held
    at the Royal Agricultural College, Cirencester on 15th-17th December 1986." ¶
    ▶  13  500     Held in December 1986. ¶
    ▶  14  504     Includes bibliographical references. ¶
    ▶  15  650  0  Coding theory ‡x Congresses. ¶
    ▶  16  650  0  Cryptography ‡x Congresses. ¶
    ▶  17  700  1  Beker, Henry. ¶
    ▶  18  700  1  Piper, F. C. ‡q (Frederick Charles), ‡d 1940- ¶
    ▶  19  710  2  Institute of Mathematics and Its Applications. ¶
```

Bibliographic record

CRYPTOGRAPHY

1986 Dec   Cirencester

Cryptography and coding -- Conference -- Papers--
Institute of Mathematics and its Applications -- [This
book is based on the proceedings of the conference]
ISBN 0198536232   **4520.784 no 20 1989**

Citation from BLDSC Index of Conference Proceedings

PREFACE

The Conference on Cryptography and Coding was held at the Royal Agricultural College, Cirencester, Gloucester on 15th - 17th December, 1986. It was sponsored and organised by the Institute of Mathematics and its Applications.

Both topics, Cryptography and Coding, are areas of mathematics that have developed with increasing momentum since their formalization by C. Shannon in the 1940s. The Communications Revolution, in particular, has made these disciplines of vital importance to modern day electronic computer networks.

Coding of information is predominantly concerned with ensuring that the data is in a form suitable for transmission and that the information can be protected from any errors that occur during its transmission. Cryptography, on the other hand, is a technique for ensuring the security of that information by ensuring its privacy, authenticity and its protection from deliberate alteration.

The aim of the Conference was to bring together mathematicians working in both cryptography and coding theory. The mathematical tools and techniques required for these two applications are similar. Yet, they tend to be treated as distinct disciplines and for many communications systems are applied as transformations to the data, in series. Within many of these applications there may be advantages in combining these processes. The result may produce both efficient and secure communications and storage of information with considerable cost benefits. This conference has begun the process of a better understanding between the cryptographers and coding theorists.

H.J. Beker   F.C. Piper
Zergo Consultants Ltd.   Royal Holloway and
                             Bedford New College.

Preface

Cryptography and coding

Based on the proceedings of a conference organized by The Institute of Mathematics and its Applications on Cryptography and Coding, held at the Royal Agricultural College, Cirencester on 15th–17th December 1986.

Edited by

HENRY J. BEKER
Zergo Consultants Ltd.

and

F. C. PIPER
Royal Holloway and Bedford New College

CLARENDON PRESS · OXFORD · 1989

Title page

Example XI. "Painleve transcendents"

Exercise:

As a cataloger, use the cover, the page facing the title page, the title page, and the t.p. verso to answer the following questions:

A. What is the main entry for this item?

B. What added entries would you make for this item?

Notes:

NATO ASI Series

Advanced Science Institutes Series

A series presenting the results of activities sponsored by the NATO Science Committee, which aims at the dissemination of advanced scientific and technological knowledge, with a view to strengthening links between scientific communities.

The series is published by an international board of publishers in conjunction with the NATO Scientific Affairs Division.

| A | Life Sciences | Plenum Publishing Corporation |
| B | Physics | New York and London |

C	Mathematical and Physical Sciences	Kluwer Academic Publishers
D	Behavioral and Social Sciences	Dordrecht, Boston, and London
E	Applied Sciences	

F	Computer and Systems Sciences	Springer-Verlag
G	Ecological Sciences	Berlin, Heidelberg, New York, London,
H	Cell Biology	Paris, Tokyo, Hong Kong, and Barcelona
I	Global Environmental Change	

Recent Volumes in this Series

Volume 278—Painlevé Transcendents
edited by Decio Levi and Pavel Winternitz

Volume 279—Fundamental Aspects of Inert Gases in Solids
edited by S. E. Donnelly and J. H. Evans

Volume 280—Chaos, Order, and Patterns
edited by Roberto Artuso, Predrag Cvitanović, and Giulio Casati

Volume 281—Low-Dimensional Structures in Semiconductors: From Basic
Physics to Applications
edited by A. R. Peaker and H. G. Grimmeiss

Volume 282—Quantum Measurements in Optics
edited by Paolo Tombesi and Daniel F. Walls

Volume 283—Cluster Models for Surface and Bulk Phenomena
edited by Gianfranco Pacchioni, Paul S. Bagus, and Fulvio Parmigiani

Volume 284—Asymptotics beyond All Orders
edited by Harvey Segur, Saleh Tanveer, and Herbert Levine

Series B: Physics

Page facing title page

Painlevé Transcendents

Their Asymptotics and
Physical Applications

Edited by

Decio Levi and
Pavel Winternitz

NATO ASI Series

Series B: Physics Vol. 278

Cover

Proceedings of a NATO Advanced Research Workshop
on Painlevé Transcendents: Their Asymptotics and Physical Applications,
held September 3–7, 1990,
in Sainte-Adèle, Québec, Canada

ISBN 0-306-44080-4

Title page verso

Painlevé Transcendents

Their Asymptotics and Physical Applications

Edited by

Decio Levi
Università degli Studi di Roma "La Sapienza"
Rome, Italy

and

Pavel Winternitz
Université de Montréal
Montréal, Québec, Canada

Plenum Press
New York and London
Published in cooperation with NATO Scientific Affairs Division

Title page

```
     OCLC:   25281832          Rec stat:    c
     Entered:   19920115       Replaced:    19960228      Used:      19960228
 ▶ Type:  a     ELvl:      Srce:       Audn:       Ctrl:       Lang:  eng
    BLvl:  m     Form:      Conf:  1    Biog:       MRec:       Ctry:  nyu
                 Cont:  b    GPub:       Fict:  0    Indx:  1
    Desc:  a     Ills:  a    Fest:  0    DtSt:  s    Dates: 1992,      ¶
 ▶   1   010     92-1169//r962 ¶
 ▶   2   040     DLC ǂc DLC ǂd UKM ¶
 ▶   3   015     GB92-46197 ¶
 ▶   4   019     27070440 ¶
 ▶   5   020     0306440504 ¶
 ▶   6   050 00  QC20.7.D5 ǂb P35 1992 ¶
 ▶   7   082 00  530.1/55352 ǂ2 20 ¶
 ▶   8   090     ǂb  ¶
 ▶   9   049     CLUM ¶
 ▶  10   245 00  Painlev´e transcendents : ǂb their asymptotics and physical
     applications / ǂc edited by Decio Levi and Pavel Winternitz. ¶
 ▶  11   260     New York : ǂb Plenum Press, ǂc c1992. ¶
 ▶  12   300     xxvi, 446 p. : ǂb ill. ; ǂc 26 cm. ¶
 ▶  13   490 1   NATO ASI series. Series B, Physics ; ǂv vol. 278 ¶
 ▶  14   500     "Published in cooperation with NATO Scientific Affairs
     Division." ¶
 ▶  15   500     "Proceedings of a NATO Advanced Research Workshop on Painlev´e
     Transcendents: Their Asymptotics and Physical Applications, held September 3-7,
     1990, in Sainte-Ad`ele, Qu´ebec, Canada"--Verso t.p. ¶
 ▶  16   504     Includes bibliographical references and indexes. ¶
 ▶  17   650 0   Painlev´e equations ǂx Congresses. ¶
 ▶  18   650 0   Mathematical physics ǂx Asymptotic theory ǂx Congresses. ¶
 ▶  19   653 0   Physics ǂa Differential equations ¶
 ▶  20   700 1   Levi, Decio. ¶
 ▶  21   700 1   Winternitz, Pavel. ¶
 ▶  22   710 2   North Atlantic Treaty Organization. ǂb Scientific Affairs
     Division. ¶
 ▶  23   711 2   NATO Advanced Research Workshop on Painlev´e Transcendents:
     Their Asymptotics and Physical Applications ǂd (1990 : ǂc Sainte-Ad`ele,
     Qu´ebec) ¶
 ▶  24   830 0   NATO ASI series. ǂn Series B, ǂp Physics ; ǂv v. 278. ¶
```

Bibliographic record

PAINLEVE TRANSCENDENTS
1990 Sep   Sainte-Adele, Canada
Painleve transcendents -- their
  asymptotics and physical appli-
cations -- NATO Advanced
  Research Workshop-- Papers
ISBN 030644-0504
        6033.64871 vol 278 1992

BLDSC Index to Conference Proceedings

9/30-2334   Montreal, PQ, CAN
**Painleve transcendents: their
asymptotics & physical appli-
cations, NATO Advanced
research workshop**
Sp: North Atlantic Treaty Organiza-
zation (NATO)
(NATO advanced science inst. ser. B,
Physics, Vol. 278)
Ed. Decio Levi & Pavel Winternitz
Pub. Plenum Press
$125.00 1992 ISBN 0-306-44050-4

InterDok citation

Example XII. "Reliability physics"

Exercise:

A. Look at the citations to the 1991 and 1992 conferences. In catalogs with which you are familiar, how would you search for the published proceedings? List as many possibilities as you can think of.

    1991 conference

    1992 conference

B. What would you expect the main entry to be for each conference?

    1991 conference

    1992 conference

C. Would you prefer to have found a serial record rather than a monograph record for this conference in your catalog? Why or why not?

Notes:

> 4/91-0152   **Las Vegas, NV, USA**
> **Reliability physics, 29th Annual symp.**
> **Sp:** IEEE Electron Devices Society
> **Sp:** IEEE Reliability Society
> Ti: Reliability physics 1991
> **Pub:** IEEE
> $70.00 1991 LC82-64313 (IEEE cat. no. 91CH2974-4)
> ISBN 0-87942-680-2 367p.

1991 conference: InterDok citation

> **RELIABILITY PHYSICS**
> 1991 Apr   Las Vegas, NV
> **Reliability physics** -- 29th Annual international symposium
> -- Papers -- Institute of Electrical and Electronics Engineers,
> Electron Devices Society -- Institute of Electrical and Electronics
> Engineers, Reliability Society-- [53 papers, IEEE cat. no.
> 91CH2974-4]
> *ISBN 0879426802 pbk, 0879426810, 0879426829*
> *microfiche*   **7356.423 29th 1991**

1991 conference: BLDSC Index of Conference Proceedings citation

> CONFERENCE PAPER
> Kageyama, M.; Hashimoto, K.; Onoda, H.
>   Formation of texture controlled aluminum and its migration performance
> Al-Si/TiN stacked structure.
> IN: 29th Annual Proceedings. Reliability Physics 1991 (Cat. No.91CH2974-4).
> (29th Annual Proceedings. Reliability Physics 1991 (Cat. No.91CH2974-4),
> Las Vegas, NV, USA. 9-11 April 1991). New York, NY, USA:
> IEEE, 1991. p. 97-101.

1991 conference: INSPEC citation

> [3]   D. L. Crook. Detecting Oxide Quality Problems using JT
>   Testing. In *Proceedings of the International Reliability*
>   *Physics Symposium*, pages 337-341, 1991

1991 conference: Citation from bibliography in published article

RELIABILITY PHYSICS
1992   Mar   San Diego, CA
Reliability physics -- 30th Annual international symposium
-- Papers -- Institute of Electrical and Electronics Engineers,
Electron Devices Society -- Institute of Electrical and Electronics
Engineers, Reliability Society-- [IEEE cat. no. 92CH3084-1]
ISBN 078030473X softbound, 0780304748 casebound,
0780304756 microfiche   **7356.423 30th 1992**

1992 conference: BLDSC Index of Conference Proceedings citation

04291933   INSPEC Abstract Number: 89301-2530F-012
Title: The effect of surface roughness of Si/sub 3/N/sub 4/ films on TDDB
characteristics of ONO films
Author(s): Tanaka, H.; Uchida, H.; Hirashita, N.; Ajioka, T.
Author Affiliation: Oki Electric Ind. Co. Lt., Tokyo, Japan
Conference Title: 30th Annual Proceedings, Reliability Physics 1992
(Cat. No.92CH3084-1) p.31-6
Published: IEEE, New York, NY, USA
Publication Date: 1992 Country of Publication: USA   x+404 pp.
ISBN 0 7803 0473 X
U.S. Copyright Clearance Center Code: CH3084-1/92/0000-0031$01.00
Conference Sponsor: IEEE
Conference Date: 31 March-2 April 1992 Conference Location: San Diego, CA, USA
Language: English

1992 conference: INSPEC citation

03560339   E.I. Monthly No: EIM9302-008768
Title: The effect of surface roughness of Si//3N//4 films on TDDB characteristics
of ONO films.
Author: Tanaka, Hiroyuki; Uchida, Hidetsugu;   Hirashita, Norio; Ajioka, Tsuneo
Conference Title: Proceedings of the 30th Annual International Reliability
Physics Symposium
Conference Location: San Diego, CA, USA   Conference Date: 1992 Mar 31-Apr 2
E.I. Conference No.: 17398
Source: Annual Proceedings - Reliability Physics (Symposium). Publ by IEEE,
IEEE Service Center, Piscataway, NJ, USA (IEEE cat n 92CH3084-1) p 31-36
Publication year: 1992
CODEN: ARLPBI   ISSN: 0099-9512   ISBN: 0-7803-0473-X
Language: English

1992 conference: COMPENDEX citation

```
        OCLC:  23956620           Rec stat:    n
        Entered:   19910619       Replaced:    19950609     Used:    19950811
►  Type:  a      ELvl:  I     Srce:  d     Audn:        Ctrl:        Lang:  eng
   BLvl:  m      Form:        Conf:  1     Biog:        MRec:        Ctry:  nyu
                 Cont:  b     GPub:        Fict:  0     Indx:  0
   Desc:  a      Ills:  a     Fest:  0     DtSt:  s     Dates:  1991,    ¶
►   1   010     ‡z 82-640313 ¶
►   2   040     RRR ‡c RRR ¶
►   3   020     0879426802 (paper) ¶
►   4   020     0879426810 (hard) ¶
►   5   020     0879426829 (microfiche) ¶
►   6   090     TK7870 ‡b .I578 1991 ¶
►   7   090     ‡b  ¶
►   8   049     CLUM ¶
►   9   111 2   International Reliability Physics Symposium ‡n (29th : ‡d 1991 :
   ‡c Las Vegas, Nev.) ¶
►  10   245 10  Reliability physics 1991 : ‡b 29th annual proceedings, Las
   Vegas, Nevadaa, April 9, 10, 11, 1991 / ‡c sponsored by the IEEE Electron
   Devices Society and the IEEE Reliability Society. ¶
►  11   260     New York, NY : ‡b Electron Device[s] Society and Reliability
   Society of the Institute of Electrical and Electronics Engineers, ‡c c1991. ¶
►  12   300     viii, 367 p. : ‡b ill. ; ‡c 28 cm. ¶
►  13   500     "IEEE catalog no. 91CH2974-4." ¶
►  14   504     Includes bibliographical references. ¶
►  15   650  0  Electronic apparatus and appliances ‡x Reliability ‡x
   Congresses. ¶
►  16   710 2   IEEE Electron Devices Society. ¶
►  17   710 2   IEEE Reliability Society. ¶
```

1991 conference: bibliographic record

```
        ARN:   309432
        Rec stat: c        Entered:      19790912
►  Type:       z    Upd status: a    Enc lvl:   n    Source:
   Roman:      ■    Ref status: a    Mod rec:        Name use: a
   Govt agn:   ■    Auth status: a   Subj:      a    Subj use: a
   Series:     n    Auth/ref:   a    Geo subd:  n    Ser use:  b
   Ser num:    n    Name:       n    Subdiv tp: ■    Rules:    c ¶
►   1   010     n 79076760  ¶
►   2   040     DLC ‡c DLC ‡d NjP ¶
►   3   005     19910730060347.4 ¶
►   4   111 20  International Reliability Physics Symposium ¶
►   5   411 20  IRPS ¶
►   6   411 20  I.R.P.S. ¶
►   7   411 20  Reliability Physics Symposium, International ¶
►   8   511 20  Reliability Physics Symposium ‡w a ¶
►   9   670     Its Reliability physics 1974, 1974. ¶
►  10   675     Reliability Physics Symposium. Annual Reliability Physics
   Symposium proceedings, 6th (1967). ¶
```

Authority record for the conference name

```
   OCLC:  25919102          Rec stat:     n
   Entered:   19920601        Replaced:    19950528      Used:    19960108
▶  Type:  a    ELvl:  I    Srce:  d    Audn:        Ctrl:         Lang:  eng
   BLvl:  m    Form:       Conf:  1    Biog:        MRec:         Ctry:  nyu
               Cont:  b    GPub:       Fict:  0     Indx:  0
   Desc:  a    Ills:  a    Fest:  0    DtSt:  s     Dates: 1992,     ¶
▶   1  010    ≠z 82-640313 ¶
▶   2  040    RRR ≠c RRR ¶
▶   3  020    078030473X (softbound) ¶
▶   4  020    0780304748 (casebound) ¶
▶   5  020    0780304756 (microfiche) ¶
▶   6  090    TK7870 ≠b .R45 1992 ¶
▶   7  049    CLUM ¶
▶   8  245 00 Reliability physics 1992 : ≠b 30th annual proceedings, San
Diego, California, March 31, April 1, 2, 1992 / ≠c sponsored by the IEEE
Electron Devices Society and the IEEE Reliability Society. ¶
▶   9  260    New York, NY : ≠b Electron Devices Society and Reliability
Society of the Institute of Electrical and Electronics Engineers, ≠c c1992. ¶
▶  10  300    x, 404 p. : ≠b ill. ; ≠c 28 cm. ¶
▶  11  500    Papers presented at the 1992 International Reliability Physics
Symposium. ¶
▶  12  500    "IEEE catalog no. 92CH3084-1." ¶
▶  13  504    Includes bibliographical references. ¶
▶  14  650  0 Electronic apparatus and appliances ≠x Reliability ≠x
Congresses. ¶
▶  15  711 2  International Reliability Physics Symposium ≠n (30th : ≠d 1992 :
≠c San Diego, Calif.) ¶
▶  16  710 2  IEEE Electron Devices Society. ¶
▶  17  710 2  IEEE Reliability Society. ¶
```

Bibliographic record for 1992 conference (record altered; may not match OCLC version)

```
   OCLC:   3766693           Rec stat:     c
   Entered:   19780331·      Replaced:     19950530      Used:      19960404
▶ Type:  a     ELvl:         Srce:  d    GPub:         Ctrl:        Lang:   eng
   BLvl:  s     Form:         Conf:  1    Freq:  a      MRec:        Ctry:   nyu
   S/L:   0     Orig:         EntW:        Regl:  r      ISSN:  1     Alph:   a
   Desc:  a     SrTp:         Cont:        DtSt:  d      Dates: 1970,1993 ¶
▶  1   010     82-640313//r95 ‡z 76-180194 ¶
▶  2   040     TOL ‡c TOL ‡d DLC ‡d NSD ‡d NST ‡d DLC ‡d NST ‡d AIP ‡d NST ‡d
OCL ‡d IUL ‡d NST ‡d OCL ‡d NST ‡d OCL ‡d NST ‡d MYG ‡d DLC ‡d NSD ¶
▶  3   012     2 ‡b 3 ‡l b ¶
▶  4   019     10199853 ‡a 13790480 ‡a 14121284 ¶
▶  5   022 0   0735-0791 ¶
▶  6   042     lc ‡a nsdp ¶
▶  7   050 00  TK7870 ‡b .S95 ¶
▶  8   082 0   621.381 ‡2 19 ¶
▶  9   090     ‡b  ¶
▶  10  049     CLUM ¶
▶  11  111 2   International Reliability Physics Symposium. ¶
▶  12  210 0   Reliab. phys. ¶
▶  13  222  0  Reliability physics ¶
▶  14  245 10  Reliability physics. ¶
▶  15  260     New York, N.Y. : ‡b Electron Devices and Reliability Societies
of the Institute of Electrical and Electronics Engineers, ‡c   -c1993. ¶
▶  16  300     v. : ‡b ill. ; ‡c 28 cm. ¶
▶  17  310     Annual ¶
▶  18  362 1   Began with vol. for 1970. ¶
▶  19  362 0   -31st (March 23-25, 1993). ¶
▶  20  500     Description based on: 19th (Apr. 7-9, 1981). ¶
▶  21  510 1   Index to IEEE publications ‡x 0099-1368 ¶
▶  22  550     Sponsored by: the IEEE Electron Devices Society and the IEEE
Reliability Group, 1970-  ; the IEEE Electron Devices Group and the IEEE
Reliability Group, <1974-1978>; the IEEE Electron Devices Society and the IEEE
Reliability Society, <1981>-1993. ¶
▶  23  504     Includes bibliographical references. ¶
▶  24  650 0   Electronic apparatus and appliances ‡x Reliability ‡x
Congresses. ¶
▶  25  650 0   Electronic apparatus and appliances ‡x Testing ‡x Congresses. ¶
▶  26  650 0   Integrated circuits ‡x Reliability ‡x Congresses. ¶
▶  27  650 0   Integrated circuits ‡x Testing ‡x Congresses. ¶
▶  28  710 2   IEEE Electron Devices Society. ¶
▶  29  710 2   IEEE Reliability Group. ¶
▶  30  710 2   IEEE Reliability Society. ¶
▶  31  710 2   Institute of Electrical and Electronics Engineers. ‡b Electron
Devices Group. ¶
▶  32  780 00  Reliability Physics Symposium. ‡t Proceedings ¶
▶  33  785 00  ‡t IEEE international reliability physics proceedings ‡x 1082-
7285 ‡w (DLC)   95647571 ‡w (OCoLC)30847997 ¶
▶  34  850     AzU ‡a CLU-P ‡a CSt ‡a CU ‡a CU-A ‡a CU-I ‡a CU-S ‡a CaAEU ‡a
CaMWU ‡a CaNBFU ‡a CaOTU ‡a CoFS ‡a CoU ‡a DLC ‡a FU ‡a GAT ‡a ICIU ‡a IaAS ‡a
IaU ‡a InLP ‡a InU ‡a KyU ‡a LU ‡a MdU ‡a MiDW ‡a MoKL ‡a MsSM ‡a NNC ‡a NRU ‡a
NcD ‡a NcRS ‡a NjP ‡a OU ‡a OrCS ‡a PPD ‡a PU ‡a TxCM ‡a TxDaM ‡a UPB ‡a UU ‡a
ViBlbV ¶
▶  35  890     Reliability physics (International Reliability Physics
Symposium). New York, N.Y. ¶
```

Serial record for the proceedings of the conferences

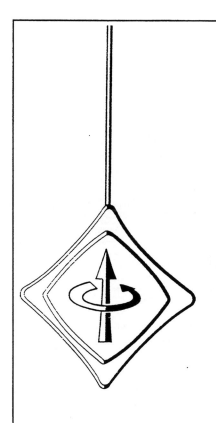

29th annual proceedings

reliability physics 1991

Las Vegas, Nevada • April 9, 10, 11, 1991

**Sponsored by
the IEEE Electron Devices Society and
the IEEE Reliability Society**

IEEE Catalog No. 91CH2974-4

1991 conference: title page

1991 INTERNATIONAL RELIABILITY PHYSICS SYMPOSIUM

SYMPOSIUM OFFICERS

GENERAL CHAIR	P. E. Kennedy, *Management Sciences*
VICE GENERAL CHAIR	H. A. Schafft, *NIST*
SECRETARY	A. K. Goel, *Elite Microelectronics*
FINANCE	D. S. Gibson, *Harris*

SYMPOSIUM COMMITTEE CHAIRS

TECHNICAL PROGRAM	D. A. Baglee, *Intel*
PUBLICITY	R. C. Blish, II, *Intel*
REGISTRATION	D. J. LaCombe, *General Electric*
ARRANGEMENTS	J. W. McPherson, *Texas Instruments*
AUDIO-VISUAL	D. Feliciano-Welpe, *Oneida Research Services*
PUBLICATIONS	G. Riga, *Riga Analytical Lab*
EQUIPMENT DEMONSTRATIONS	P.J. Boudreaux, *DOD*
TUTORIAL	J. Klema, *Motorola*
WORKSHOPS	J. T. Yue, *AMD*
CONSULTANT	R. C. Walker, *SAR Associates*
CONSULTANT	D. F. Barber, *Scien-Tech Associates*

BOARD OF DIRECTORS

B. L. Euzent *Intel*	H. A. Schafft *NIST*
L. A. Kasprzak *IBM*	W. H. Schroen *Texas Instruments*
P. E. Kennedy *Management Sciences*	R. W. Thomas *Rome Laboratory*
N. McAfee *Westinghouse Electric Co.*	M. H. Woods *Intel*

Published by the

ELECTRON DEVICE SOCIETY AND RELIABILITY SOCIETY

of the

INSTITUTE OF ELECTRICAL AND ELECTRONICS ENGINEERS, INC.

IEEE Catalog No. 91CH2974-4
Library of Congress Catalog No. 82-640313
ISBN: 0-87942-680-2 Soft Cover
ISBN: 0-87942-681-0 Hard Cover
ISBN: 0-87942-682-9 Microfiche

1991 conference: title page verso

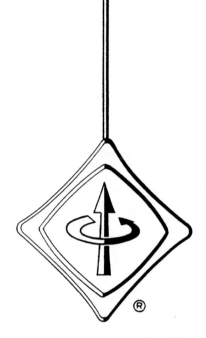

30th annual proceedings

reliability physics 1992

San Diego, California • March 31, April 1, 2, 1992

**Sponsored by
the IEEE Electron Devices Society and
the IEEE Reliability Society**

IEEE Catalog No. 92CH3084-1

1992 conference: title page

1992 INTERNATIONAL RELIABILITY PHYSICS SYMPOSIUM

SYMPOSIUM OFFICERS

GENERAL CHAIR..H. A. Schafft, *NIST*
VICE GENERAL CHAIR .... D. A. Baglee, *Intel*
SECRETARY.. W. R. Hunter, *Texas Instruments*
FINANCE...S. K. Groothuis, *Texas Instruments*

SYMPOSIUM COMMITTEE CHAIRS

TECHNICAL PROGRAM ....R. C. Blish, II, *Intel*
PUBLICITY...A. G. Rawers, *Integrated Informationl*
REGISTRATION ....J. G. Cottle, *University South Florida*
ARRANGEMENTS ....A. K. Goel, *Elite Microelectronics*
AUDIO-VISUAL...W. K. Gladden, *Advance Micro Devices*
PUBLICATIONS .... D. J. LaCombe, *General Electric*
EQUIPMENT DEMONSTRATIONS.................J. W. McPherson, *Texas Instruments*
TUTORIAL.. A. N. Campbell, *Sandia National Laboratories*
WORKSHOPS.. G. Riga, *Riga Analytical Lab*
CONSULTANT... R. C. Walker, *SAR Associates*
CONSULTANT.. D. F. Barber, *Scien-Tech Associates*

BOARD OF DIRECTORS

D. A. Baglee   H. A. Schafft
Intel   *NIST*

L. A. Kasprzak   W. H. Schroen
IBM   *Texas Instruments*

P. E. Kennedy   R. W. Thomas
Management Sciences   *Rome Laboratory*

N. McAfee   M. H. Woods
Westinghouse Electric Co.   *Intel*

Published by the

ELECTRON DEVICE SOCIETY AND RELIABILITY SOCIETY

of the

INSTITUTE OF ELECTRICAL AND ELECTRONICS ENGINEERS, INC.

IEEE Catalog No.   92CH3084-1
Library of Congress No.   82-640313   Serial
ISBN: 0-7803-0473-x   Softbound
                          0-7803-0474-8   Casebound
                          0-7803-0475-6   Microfiche

ii

1992 conference: title page verso

Example XIII. "Ferroelectricity"

Exercise:

Look at the citations given below:

1. From the IEEE index to its publications

> **Ferroelectricity, 5th International Meeting on,** (IMF-5),
> held Aug. 17-21, 1981 in University Park, PA; sponsored by IUPAP,
> ONR, ARO, NSF, IEEE, et al. *Proceedings,* 1272 pp.

2. From INSPEC

> CONFERENCE PAPER
> Toledano, J.-C.
>   Symmetry aspects of structural phase transitions. (5th
>   International Meeting on Ferroelectricity (IMF-5),
>   University Park, PA, USA, 17-21 Aug. 1981).
> Ferroelectrics, Oct. 1981, vol.35, (no.1-4):31-6.

The proceedings of this conference were issued in two different covers: as a monograph by IEEE, and as an issue of the serial *Ferroelectrics*. Look at the LC bibliographic record, at the title page and title page verso that apply to both issues, and at the cover of the serial issue. How would a record describing the proceedings as part of the journal *Ferroelectrics* be different from the LC record?

Notes:

```
        OCLC:  8729862              Rec stat:     c
        Entered:   19820715        Replaced:     19841129      Used:      19950803
    ▶   Type:  a    ELvl:           Srce:         Audn:         Ctrl:          Lang:   eng
        BLvl:  m    Form:           Conf:  1      Biog:         MRec:          Ctry:   nyu
                    Cont:  b        GPub:         Fict:  0      Indx:  0
        Desc:  a    Ills:  a        Fest:  0      DtSt:  s      Dates: 1981,     ¶
    ▶   1   010      82-151594 ¶
    ▶   2   040      DLC ǂc DLC ǂd OCL ǂd KKU ǂd MNU ¶
    ▶   3   019      8185768 ǂa 10392015 ¶
    ▶   4   050 0    QC596 ǂb .I57 1981 ¶
    ▶   5   082 0    537/.2448 ǂ2 19 ¶
    ▶   6   090      ǂb  ¶
    ▶   7   049      CLUM ¶
    ▶   8   111 2    International Meeting on Ferroelectricity ǂn (5th : ǂd 1981 : ǂc
        Pennsylvania State University) ¶
    ▶   9   245 14   The Fifth International Meeting on Ferroelectricity, IMF-5, 17-
        21 August 1981, the Pennsylvania State University, USA / ǂc sponsors, the
        International Union of Pure and Applied Physics (IUPAP) in cooperation with the
        Office of Naval Research (ONR) ... [at al.]. ¶
    ▶   10  260      [New York, N.Y. : ǂb Institute of Electrical and Electronics
        Engineers, ǂc 1981?] ¶
    ▶   11  300      xxx, 1272 p. : ǂb ill. ; ǂc 27 cm. ¶
    ▶   12  500      "81CH1641-0"--Spine. ¶
    ▶   13  504      Includes bibliographical references. ¶
    ▶   14  650  0   Ferroelectricity ǂx Congresses. ¶
    ▶   15  710 2    International Union of Pure and Applied Physics. ¶
```

Bibliographic record (record altered; may not match OCLC version)

THE FIFTH INTERNATIONAL
MEETING ON FERROELECTRICITY, IMF-5

17-21 August 1981
The Pennsylvania State University, USA

PART 1

Sponsors: The International Union of Pure and Applied Physics
—(IUPAP) in cooperation with

The Office of Naval Research (ONR)
The Army Research Office (ARO)
The National Science Foundation (NSF)
The Institute of Electrical and Electronic Engineers (IEEE)
The American Ceramic Society (ACS)
International Rockwell Company
North American Philips Company
Gordon and Breach Science Publishers Ltd.

Title page of both the IEEE and *Ferroelectrics* publications

NOTE ON PAGINATION

The Proceedings of the Fifth International Meeting on Ferroelectricity are being
published as 5 consecutive volumes of FERROELECTRICS (Volumes 35 to 39).

To facilitate indexing and referring to these proceedings, the page numbers run
continuously through all five Volumes. A complete table of contents is included at
the beginning and an author index at the end of each volume.

T.p. verso of both the IEEE and *Ferroelectrics* publications

Volume 35, Numbers 1/2/3/4 (1981)   FEROA 8 35(1/2/3/4) 1–270 (1981)
ISSN: 0015–0193

FERROELECTRICS

The international journal devoted to the theoretical, experimental, and applied aspects of ferroelectrics and related materials

Proceedings of the Fifth International Meeting on Ferroelectricity, Pennsylvania State University, U.S.A., August 1981

Guest Editor: Gerhard R. Barsch

Part 1

GORDON AND BREACH SCIENCE PUBLISHERS   New York/ London/ Paris

Cover of *Ferroelectrics*

Example XIV. "Solar engineering 1986"

Exercise:

A. Based on the citations given on the next page, in catalogs with which you are familiar, how would you search for the published proceedings? List as many possibilities as you can think of.

B. Look at the bibliographic record that follows the citations. Would you have found this record?

Notes:

1986 Apr   Anaheim, CA
Solar engineering -- 8th Annual solar energy conference
-- Papers -- ASME, Solar Energy Division
8327.20148 8th 1986

BLDSC Index of Conference Proceedings (under SOLAR ENGINEERING)

01839957   NOV-85-019073; EDB-86-163840
Title: results from operation of the Crosbyton solar bowl
Author(s): O'Hair, E.A.; Simpson, T.L.; Green, B.; Ferber, R.R.
Affiliation: Crosbyton Solar Power Project, Dept. of Electrical
    Engineering, Texas Tech Univ., Lubbock, TX
Title: Solar engineering - 1986
Conference title: ASME Solar Energy Division conference
Conference location: Anaheim, CA, USA   Conference date: 14 Apr 1986
Publisher: American Society of Mechanical Engineers, New York, NY
Publication date: 1986   p. 205-209
Report Number(s):   CONF-860406-
Language: English

DOE

02136566   E.I. Monthly No: EIM8612-084236
Title: RESULTS FROM OPERATION OF THE CROSBYTON SOLAR BOWL.
Author: O'Hair, E. A.; Simpson, T. L.; Green, B.
Corporate Source: Texas Tech Univ, Lubbock, TX , USA
Conference Title: Solar Engineering - 1986, Proceedings of the ASME Solar Energy
    Conference (SED Eighth Annual Conference)
Conference Location: Anaheim, CA, USA Conference Date: 1986 Apr 13-16
E.I. Conference No.: 08768
Source: Solar Engineering 1986. Publ. by ASME, New York, NY, USA p. 205-209
Publication year: 1986
CODEN: SOLEDS   ISSN: 0734-7472
Language: English

COMPENDEX

```
      OCLC:  8809691          Rec stat:    c
      Entered:    19820927    Replaced:    19950309     Used:      19960326
   ▶  Type:  a    ELvl:        Srce:  d    GPub:        Ctrl:        Lang:   eng
      BLvl:  s    Form:        Conf:  1    Freq:  a     MRec:        Ctry:   nyu
      S/L:   0    Orig:        EntW:        Regl:  r     ISSN:  1     Alph:   a
      Desc:  a    SrTp:        Cont:        DtSt:  c     Dates: 19uu,9999 ¶
   ▶   1   010      83-643833 ≠z sn82-6955 ¶
   ▶   2   040      NSD ≠c NSD ≠d DLC ≠d NSD ≠d DLC ≠d AIP ≠d NST ≠d AGL ¶
   ▶   3   012      2 ≠b 3 ¶
   ▶   4   022 0    0734-7472 ¶
   ▶   5   030      SOLEDS ¶
   ▶   6   042      1c ≠a nsdp ¶
   ▶   7   050 00   TJ810 ≠b .A462a ¶
   ▶   8   070 0    TJ810.A462 ¶
   ▶   9   072 0    P130 ≠a X600 ¶
   ▶  10   082 0    621.47/05 ≠2 19 ¶
   ▶  11   090      ≠b  ¶
   ▶  12   049      CLUM ¶
   ▶  13   110 2    American Society of Mechanical Engineers. ≠b Solar Energy
      Division. ≠b Conference. ¶
   ▶  14   210 0    Solar eng. ≠b (New York, N.Y.) ¶
   ▶  15   222 0    Solar engineering ≠b (New York, N.Y.) ¶
   ▶  16   245 10   Solar engineering / ≠c presented at proceedings of the ASME
      Solar Energy Division ... Annual Conference. ¶
   ▶  17   260      New York, N.Y. : ≠b American Society of Mechanical Engineers, ¶
   ▶  18   265      American Society of Mechanical Engineers, 345 E. 47th St., New
      York, NY 10017 ¶
   ▶  19   300      v. : ≠b ill. ; ≠c 28 cm. ¶
   ▶  20   310      Annual ¶
   ▶  21   500      Description based on: 3rd (1981). ¶
   ▶  22   510 2    Engineering index annual (1968) ≠x 0360-8557 ¶
   ▶  23   510 2    Engineering index monthly (1984) ≠x 0742-1974 ¶
   ▶  24   510 2    Engineering index bioengineering abstracts ≠x 0736-6213 ¶
   ▶  25   510 2    Engineering index energy abstracts ≠x 0093-8408 ¶
   ▶  26   650  0   Solar energy ≠x Periodicals. ¶
   ▶  27   710 2    American Society of Mechanical Engineers. ¶
   ▶  28   850      AAP ≠a AU ≠a CSt ≠a CU ≠a CU-A ≠a CoU ≠a DLC ≠a DNAL ≠a GAT ≠a
      IaAS ≠a IaU ≠a InLP ≠a MiU ≠a MnU ≠a NBuU-SE ≠a NSyU ≠a NcD ≠a OU ≠a OrCS ≠a
      ViBlbV ¶
   ▶  29   890      Solar engineering (American Society of Mechanical Engineers.
      Solar Energy Division. Conference) ¶
   ▶  30   936      8th 1986 LIC ¶
```

Bibliographic record

```
   ARN:    920006
   Rec stat: c       Entered:       19830609
▶  Type:     z        Upd status:  a     Enc lvl:   n      Source:
   Roman:    ■        Ref status:  a     Mod rec:          Name use: a
   Govt agn: ■        Auth status: a     Subj:      a      Subj use: a
   Series:   n        Auth/ref:    a     Geo subd:  n      Ser use:  b
   Ser num:  n        Name:        n     Subdiv tp: ■      Rules:    c ¶
▶   1  010      n  83029200 ¶
▶   2  040      DLC ≠c DLC ≠d DLC ¶
▶   3  005      19890707133400.4 ¶
▶   4  110 20   American Society of Mechanical Engineers. ≠b Solar Energy
Division. ≠b Conference ¶
▶   5  411 20   ASME Solar Energy Conference (1982- ) ¶
▶   6  411 20   ASME Solar Energy Division Conference ¶
▶   7  411 20   ASME Energy Conference ¶
▶   8  410 20   American Society of Mechanical Engineers. ≠b Solar Energy
Division. ≠b Technical Conference ¶
▶   9  411 20   SED Conference ¶
▶  10  511 20   Conference on Systems Simulation, Economic Analysis/Solar
Heating and Cooling Operational Results ≠n (3rd : ≠d 1981 : ≠c Reno, Nev.) ≠w
a ¶
▶  11 [1] 670      Its Solar engineering, 1983: ≠b t.p. (ASME Solar Energy
Division ... Annual Conference) p. iii (ASME Solar Energy Division Conference
is an outgrowth of two conferences: conference on Systems Simulation and
Economic Analysis for Solar Heating and Cooling (1st held June 1978, 2nd, Jan.
1980) and conference on Solar Heating and Cooling Systems Operational Results
(1st held Nov. 1978, 2nd, Nov. 1979) which merged in 1981 as Third Annual
Systems Simulation and Economic Analysis/Solar Heating and Cooling Operational
Results Conference (Apr. 1981). Since 1981 shortened to ASME Solar Energy ¶
▶  11 [2] 670      Division Fourth Annual Technical Conference (Albuquerque,
1982) and this designtion will continue; fifth annual Solar Energy Division
Technical Conference; 1983 ASME Solar Energy Conference) its Solar engineering,
1986: t.p. (ASME Solar Energy Conference (SED Eighth Annual Conference) p. iii
(8th Annual ASME Energy Conference) ¶
```

Authority record

SOLAR
ENGINEERING – 1986

PROCEEDINGS OF THE ASME
SOLAR ENERGY CONFERENCE
(SED EIGHTH ANNUAL CONFERENCE)

ANAHEIM, CALIFORNIA
APRIL 13–16, 1986

sponsored by
THE SOLAR ENERGY DIVISION, ASME

edited by
R. R. FERBER
JET PROPULSION LABORATORY

THE AMERICAN SOCIETY OF MECHANICAL ENGINEERS
United Engineering Center   345 East 47th Street   New York, N.Y. 10017

Title page

FOREWORD

Over the past few years priorities in solar energy research have changed because of changes in government funding, commercialization of certain technologies and because of experiences gained. More recently, the discontinuance of the Federal solar energy tax credits at the end of 1985 has significantly changed the economics of application for solar technologies. Further changes in application economics are being brought about as a result of the decline of oil prices in the January — February, 1986 time period. The future economics of solar technologies is addressed head-on by the conference opening panel session on Monday, April 14, 1986. The directions and trends in the solar energy research and applications can be seen from the papers presented at the annual ASME Solar Energy Conference and from the additional program panel sessions being presented by twenty distinguished panelists appearing in four different panel sessions on timely and important solar topics. This Conference has become known for the high standards of papers on progress in solar energy engineering. The high standard of the papers is maintained by the active participation of the Solar Energy Division technical committees and the ASME paper review process. Each paper is subjected to critical peer reviews, and a number of papers have to undergo considerable revision before being accepted. The papers presented in this Conference are also considered for publication in the ASME transactions-Journal of Solar Energy Engineering.

In the 8th Annual ASME Energy Conference, there are 80 papers in 13 sessions plus the four panel sessions. The sessions were sponsored and organized by the ASME Solar Energy Division technical committees. The topics include solar energy fundamentals, testing and measurements, thermal power, photovoltaic power, space solar power, "solar bowl" technology, solar ponds, simulation and modeling, system economics, impact on utilities, industrial process heat, storage systems and heating and cooling systems.

The Conference chairmen would like to acknowledge the efforts of the session organizers and technical committee chairmen who have worked so hard to make the 1986 Conference a reality. Among them are: Ozer Arnas, Jim Chiou, Hunter Fanney, Bob Ferber, Halil Guven, Henry Healey, Hudy Hewitt, Zalman Lavan, Tom Mancini, Jeff Morehouse, Marty Murphy, Ed O'Hair, James Rogan, John Tichy, and Dan Turner. Thanks are also due to the ASME staff, especially Bill Leggitt, Marvin Spitzer, and Gemma Tansey for program arrangements and publication of the proceedings. A special thanks is due to the many reviewers who volunteered their time and expertise to review over 100 papers and helped in keeping the high standards of the papers in the proceedings. Finally, the chairmen would like to recognize the efforts of all the authors who contributed their papers for this Conference.

W. Dan Turner
General Program Chairman

Robert R. Ferber
Technical Program Chairman
1986 ASME Solar Energy Conference

iii

Foreword

APPENDIX D:
Discussion Leaders' Guide to the Workbook Examples

Sara Shatford Layne

The examples are presented in a progression from (relatively) simple to (relatively) complex. They were selected to bring out the following kinds of problems:

1. determining if a conference is named and, if so, what that name is;

2. determining the main entry for the proceedings of a conference and determining additional access points;

3. choosing between monographic and serial treatment for the proceedings of a series of conferences; and,

4. presenting, in the bibliographic record, information that is unique to conference proceedings, such as date, place, and sponsoring bodies of the conference.

Example I: This is a relatively straightforward example. The conference is clearly "named"; the name appears on the title page so it is (also clearly) the main entry; the sponsorship statement is clear. Point out that the location of the name of conference in the item determines whether the name is a main entry or added entry in the catalog record (and, therefore, where the name of the conference appears in the bibliographic description of the item.). Discuss, if desired, the possible locations in the record for the information appearing at the bottom of the title page (location and date of conference, editor information, sponsorship information) and the advantages/disadvantages of the different locations (in field 245, in field 500).

Example II: This is an example of an "unnamed" conference: the conference is not named in the item. What kinds of problems are caused by extrapolating or creating a name that does not actually appear in a bibliographic item, as was done in the *ISTP* citation?

Example III: According to both the bibliographic records and the citations, the 1988 conference is not named, while the 1991 conference *is* named (*"Winter School on Hadronic Physics"*). What are the differences between the two publications? The significant difference is the location of the name in the publication. The 1988 conference was cataloged by LC during the time that no access points were made for conferences not "prominently named." If cataloged today, the conference name would probably appear as an added entry in the record for the 1988 conference. It is interesting that citation practice appears to match the no longer current LC cataloging practice. (Note: the presence of quotation marks in *Third Winter School on "Hadronic Physics"* should not influence the decision as to whether the conference is named; LC practice is to consider capitalization but not the presence or absence of quotation marks when determining whether a conference is named.) Discuss the implications, in terms of description and access, of considering the 1988 conference to be named or unnamed.

Example IV: Point out that the citation lacks an article title and page numbers and does not match the actual title of the proceedings. Such citations are not uncommon and are frequently based on attendance at a conference where a paper is presented rather than on the published proceedings. Discuss the importance of authority records and the references generated by them in identifying the name of a conference; discuss choosing between an acronym and a spelled-out form for the name of a conference when both appear on a title page. Discuss the lack of reliability of titles as access points to conference proceedings.

Example V: Compare the choices made on the worksheets to those shown by the bibliographic and authority records. Compare them also with the various citations given. Discuss the implications of considering *Crypto '88* to be a name and of not mentioning or tracing the conference sponsors. Discuss what would be required to catalog this as a serial: LC practice (as of 1991) is to recatalog something as a serial when several sequential items have the same title (for example, *Advances in Cryptology*) and the same conference name (for example, *Crypto*). Recataloged as a serial, the bibliographic record would have the following 111 and 245 fields:

```
111 2    Crypto.
245 10   Advances in cryptology : ‡b proceedings of Crypto...
(Field 245 is based in the proceedings of the 1983 conference.)
```

Discuss advantages and disadvantages of recataloging as a serial: what information appears in the monographic records that would not appear in the serial record (for example, date, place, editors, possibly series numbers of the individual conference proceedings) and how this would affect access.

Example VI: Look at the bibliographic record and the citations to the conference. Discuss why "World Marina 1991" might not be considered a "name" while "Crypto '88" is considered a "name." (Answer: "World Marina" is not an abbreviation or initialism as "Crypto" is, so LC does not consider it to be a "name"). "World Marina '91 Conference" is a "name," but this item was cataloged by LC during the time that names not appearing "prominently" were ignored. Note that citation practice (with the exception of E.I.) appears to match cataloging practice. Discuss possible problems of "adjusting" titles to create named conferences, as was done by E.I. in this example. Discuss implications for retrieval of this record. Discuss also choices of sponsoring bodies to be transcribed and traced: the second "body" does not have a "name" (note lack of capitalization in preface) and so is not traced; the first of the "in cooperation" bodies is not traced because there are two principal bodies and more than one "collaborating" body. Discuss importance of putting date and place somewhere in the record (either as a quoted note or added on to the end of field 245). Discuss implications of either choice for retrieval and identification.

Example VII: Look at the bibliographic and authority records after answering the questions. Look also at the citations given. Consider the problems of determining what the chief source of information is in this case. This is *not* a case where the information normally found on a single title page is spread across two facing pages, which then are treated together as the chief source of information. P. [iii] is the title page. P. [ii] is the page facing the title page, and it contains information not found on the title page that may need to be accounted for in some way in the bibliographic record as it may be critical for identification and retrieval (for example, "intellectual leverage," perhaps the theme of the conference, appears to be treated as the title proper in the BLDSC citation). Consider what would need to be true for the proceedings of this conference to be cataloged as a serial (the name of conference would need to be stable, the title of proceedings would have to remain the same for several successive conferences). Consider the implications for retrieval and identification of cataloging this as a serial; what information appears in the monograph records that would not appear in the serial record (for example, date, place of the individual conference proceedings) and how this would affect access.

Example VIII: Discuss what rules and principles might have led to establishing the conference names as shown by the Library of Congress authority and bibliographic records (the choice of name follows usage in each publication). Discuss advantages and disadvantages of the Library of Congress approach. Emphasize the importance of authority records whatever approach might be taken. Note that *Astronomy & Astrophysics Abstracts* citation practice does not appear to match LC cataloging practice. Discuss also, if desired, the pros and cons of tracing the name of the corporate body sponsoring the conference separately, and in addition to, its appearance as part of the conference name (in the record for the August 1989 colloquium there is no separate access point for the International Astronomical Union; the name of the body appears in an access point only as part of the name of the conference).

Example IX: This is an example of the proceedings of a smaller conference held within, or in close association with, another, larger, conference. Note that the name of the larger conference is an added entry. Note that the form of the name of the larger conference that appears on the title page is treated as a variant, and that this treatment is justified in a note on the authority record. Note that the organizing body is traced as an added entry. Note also that the main entry used on the bibliographic record does not even appear in the BLDSC citation.

Example X: The conference is "named" in the preface, although not in the same form as in the citation, but it is not "named" in the bibliographic record. Consider the importance of catalogers seeking conference names in prefaces; consider the importance of reference librarians (and other database searchers) knowing that conference names in citations, especially those "to appear" may not coincide with bibliographic records. Common ways in which citations may differ from bibliographic records: acronyms or initialisms for corporate names may or may not form part of conference names, but the corporate name may be an access point in its own right to that record; one or more of the words in a conference name may be different; the date (or other information) may be misremembered by the person writing the citation.

Example XI: This is an example of a conference named on the title page verso and not, therefore, the main entry of the item. Conferences named elsewhere than on the chief source of information have been given added entries rather than main entries since the 1991 LCRI on this topic. (Note: the series information appears to have been taken from the cover rather than from the series title page.)

Example XII: Look at the title page and title page verso for each conference. Look also at the monographic bibliographic records: the 1991 record is cataloged according to the rules as they were before the 1991 LCRI specifying that the conference name must appear in the chief source if it is to be the main entry; the 1992 record is cataloged following the LCRI. Discuss advantages and disadvantages of this rule interpretation (think also about Example XI). LC has cataloged these proceedings as a serial. Consider the implications for retrieval and identification of cataloging this as a serial; what information appears in the monograph records that would not appear in the serial record (for example, date, place of the individual conference proceedings) and how this would affect access.

Example XIII: This is an example of the proceedings of a conference issued simultaneously as a monograph and as volumes of a serial (an "analytic"). These proceedings were issued in two different sets of covers but with identical title pages: 1) as volumes of *Ferroelectrics*, published by Gordon and Breach Science Publishers; and, 2) as a single volume issued by IEEE. A bibliographic record that described the proceedings as volumes of *Ferroelectrics* would have a different field 260 and would also have a field 440 :

```
260       New York : ‡b Gordon and Breach Science Publishers, ‡c
          1981.
440 0     Ferroelectrics, ‡x 0015-0193 ; ‡v v. 35-39
```

Discuss whether the proceedings of a conference issued both as a monograph and as volumes of a serial should be described with a single bibliographic record and the problems of doing so that are raised by this example.

Example XIV: The proceedings of this conference have been cataloged as a serial. Discuss the advantages and disadvantages to this approach. Consider, for example, the information that appears on the title page (place, date, editor), and that would appear in a monograph record, but that does not appear in the serial record. Discuss also the problems of a conference that is referred to by two different names on a title page and the importance of authority records and the references that they generate for locating the proceedings of such a conference.

Abbreviations Used in this Volume

AACR	*Anglo-American Cataloguing Rules*
AACR 1	*Anglo-American Cataloging Rules*, 1st edition (1967)
AACR 2	*Anglo-American Cataloguing Rules*, 2nd edition (1978, and 1988 revision)
ACM	Association for Computing Machinery
ACRL	Association of College and Research Libraries, a division of the American Library Association
AIAA	American Institute of Aeronautics and Astronautics
ALCTS	Association for Library Collections & Technical Services, a division of the American Library Association
ANSI	American National Standards Institute
ARL	Association of Research Libraries
ASME	American Society of Mechanical Engineers
BLDSC	British Library Document Supply Centre
CC:DA	Committee on Cataloging: Description and Access of CCS
CCS	Cataloging and Classification Section of ALCTS
CIP	cataloging-in-publication
CONSER	Cooperative Online Serials (formerly, Conversion of Serials Project)
CSB	*Cataloging Service Bulletin*
FTP	file transfer protocol
GPO	Government Printing Office (U.S.)
IEEE	Institute of Electrical and Electronics Engineers

ISBN   International Standard Book Number

ISSN   International Standard Serial Number

ISI   Institute for Scientific Information

ISTP   *Index to Scientific and Technical Proceedings*

LC   Library of Congress

LCRI, LCRIs Library of Congress Rule Interpretations

LSM   Library of Science and Medicine, Rutgers

MARC   machine-readable cataloging

NBS   National Bureau of Standards (U.S.)

NTIS   National Technical Information Service (U.S.)

OCLC   OCLC Online Computer Library Center, Inc.

OPAC   online public access catalog

PIP   *Proceedings in Print*

RLIN   Research Libraries Network

SCI   *Science Citation Index*

SME   Society of Manufacturing Engineers

STS   Science and Technology Section of ACRL

Index

(The examples in Appendix C are not indexed separately. Information covered in the examples can be retrieved through the index entries to the Discussion Guide in Appendix D)